"*Carved in Ebony* introduces the stories of Black women that for too long have been untold. With unapologetic conviction and vulnerable eloquence, Jasmine shows how their faith and steadfast purposefulness indelibly shaped our nation and world. You will be both inspired and challenged to continue the legacy these women began."

Elizabeth Woodson, institute classes and curriculum director, The Village Church

"Books are meant to shape us. While reading *Carved in Ebony*, I imagined that I was joining Jasmine Holmes on a journey looking at old truths with fresh eyes. After I was done, I realized that Jasmine wasn't using her pen just to tell a story. She was using it as a chisel. My faith and confidence in the goodness of God has been refined and polished as a result of seeing God's faithfulness in the lives of these women. I can't wait to witness the other statues she sculpts when other people get their hands on this book."

John Onwuchekwa, author, *We Go On*; cofounder, Portrait Coffee

"Too often, the stories of faithful Black women have been lost to history. Thankfully, Jasmine Holmes has done the hard work of bringing these stories to light by chasing down footnotes and searching through archives for her new book, *Carved in Ebony*. Reading these stories will encourage your faith, inspire your courage, and remind you of God's extraordinary work in the midst of the everyday faithfulness of his people."

Melissa Kruger, author and director of women's initiatives, The Gospel Coalition

"*Carved in Ebony*, like its author, is courageous, compassionate, and clear. In considering the lives and faith of the women profiled here, we can learn how we as Christians can serve Christ and love the world for which he died and lives again."

Russell Moore, public theologian, *Christianity Today*; director, *Christianity Today*'s Public Theology Project

"Jasmine Holmes dusts off the lives of ten Black women in history, placing their contributions to the world and the church squarely in our current climate and circumstances. I was convicted, comforted, and challenged by Jasmine's strong, wise, and informed voice. *Carved in Ebony* is a treasure that belongs on every shelf of American history."

Lore Ferguson Wilbert, author, *Handle with Care*

CROWNED
WITH
GLORY

JASMINE L. HOLMES'S PREVIOUS BOOKS

Carved in Ebony

Carved in Ebony, Young Reader's Edition

CROWNED
WITH
GLORY

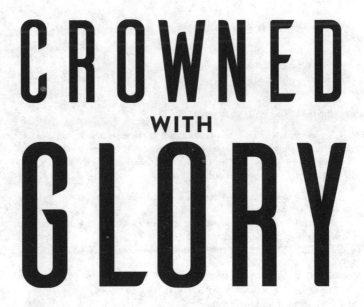

How Proclaiming *the* Truth *of* Black Dignity
Has Shaped American History

JASMINE L. HOLMES

BakerBooks
a division of Baker Publishing Group
Grand Rapids, Michigan

© 2023 by Jasmine L. Holmes

Published by Baker Books
a division of Baker Publishing Group
Grand Rapids, Michigan
www.bakerbooks.com

Printed in the United States of America

Library of Congress Cataloging-in-Publication Data
Names: Holmes, Jasmine L., 1990– author.
Title: Crowned with glory : how proclaiming the truth of Black dignity has shaped American history / Jasmine L. Holmes.
Description: Grand Rapids, Michigan : Baker Books, a division of Baker Publishing Group, [2023] | Includes bibliographical references.
Identifiers: LCCN 2022059150 | ISBN 9781540903167 (paperback) | ISBN 9781540903617 (casebound) | ISBN 9781493443246 (ebook)
Subjects: LCSH: African Americans—History. | African American Christians. United States—Race relations—History.
Classification: LCC E185 .H567 2023 | DDC 973/.0496073—dc23/eng/20230207
LC record available at https://lccn.loc.gov/2022059150

Unless otherwise indicated, Scripture quotations are from the King James Version of the Bible.

Scripture quotations labeled ESV are from The Holy Bible, English Standard Version® (ESV®), copyright © 2001 by Crossway, a publishing ministry of Good News Publishers. Used by permission. All rights reserved. ESV Text Edition: 2016

Scripture quotations labeled NIV are from THE HOLY BIBLE, NEW INTERNATIONAL VERSION®, NIV® Copyright © 1973, 1978, 1984, 2011 by Biblica, Inc.® Used by permission. All rights reserved worldwide.

Unless otherwise noted, emphases in quotations are added by the author.

The author is represented by the literary agency of The Gates Group, www.the-gates-group.com.

Baker Publishing Group publications use paper produced from sustainable forestry practices and post-consumer waste whenever possible.

23   24   25   26   27   28   29   7   6   5   4   3   2   1

For my sons—
Walter, Ezra, and Malcolm

CONTENTS

If we must die, O let us nobly die,
So that our precious blood may not be shed
In vain; then even the monsters we defy
Shall be constrained to honor us though dead!
                    —Claude McKay, "If We Must Die"

When I look at your heavens, the work of your fingers,
    the moon and the stars, which you have set in place,
what is man that you are mindful of him,
    and the son of man that you care for him?
Yet you have made him a little lower than the heavenly
        beings
    and crowned him with glory and honor.
                                    —Psalm 8:3–5 ESV

INTRODUCTION

A few years ago, at the start of the pandemic, when a national outcry arose about critical race theory being taught in schools, I stood in front of a classroom full of seniors and almost lost my cool.

At that point, I had been a teacher for nine years, nearly all of it conducted in mostly white spaces. Eight of those years were spent in either all-white classrooms or with one or two Black students per year.

My own education was very white. Despite being home-schooled, the majority of my extracurriculars and co-op spaces were white. My church was mostly white. My friends and my preteen love interests were all white too.

I was used to being the only Black girl in the room, and then I grew up and became the only Black girl *and* the only adult in many a classroom.

That day shouldn't have been all that different. I had been tasked to talk to them about the Founding Fathers and slavery. English major though I was, my teaching journey led me to begin teaching less English and more history, fueled by my own voracious reading and research as well as admins who were kind enough to let me follow my interests. Their teacher knew I had been doing a lot of research about slavery and the Founding Fathers for a book I was working on, and she asked me to share some of my findings with her class.

I talked about how these men who boasted of liberty were also slaveholders; how they created a system withholding those rights from the enslaved while speaking of the inherent rights of all men. And I'm going to be honest with you—my research failed me. Combining the last-minute invitation and my over-estimating my ability to take emotion out of this conversation, I floundered.

The students responded to my talk with statements like, "No one knew slavery was wrong back then." "Some slaves were just really happy living with their masters." "What were they even supposed to do if they got free?" "Slavery was just a normal part of life."

Afterward, I went to my car and sobbed.

I'd *never* cried after a class before.

Not once.

Not when I was teaching fifth grade and little Timmy threw something at me. Not when I asked a tenth grader to hand me his phone and he stood toe to toe with me in my third trimester and said, "Make me." Not even when I threw up in the trash can outside of a senior thesis class just as the period dismissed and all the students saw me.

But this time, I called my husband and told him, "I felt like I was defending my humanity in front of those kids."

That was the day I felt the full exhaustion of being a Black teacher in white spaces. It was also the day I felt the full extent of my own ignorance about our nation's history, and the ignorance that had been passed on to the next generation. That day I hit the wall of being the only Black teacher in the school and decided I needed to find the answers to the questions that stumped me.

I finished out the school year, got pregnant over Christmas break, and wept that summer when I finally quit because I didn't want to leave. I loved teaching. I miss it just about every day. But I felt like I loved teaching more than it loved me.

That still hurts.

I was no longer teaching by the time I read bell hooks's seminal teacher work, *Teaching to Transgress*. She described going to her all-Black elementary school this way:

> Almost all our teachers at Booker T. Washington were black women. They were committed to nurturing intellect so that we could become scholars, thinkers, and cultural workers—black folks who used our "minds." We learned early that our devotion to learning, to a life of the mind, was a counter-hegemonic act, a fundamental way to resist every strategy of white racist colonization. Though they did not define or articulate these practices in theoretical terms, my teachers were enacting a revolutionary pedagogy of resistance that was profoundly anticolonial. Within these segregated schools, black children who were deemed exceptional, gifted, were given special care. Teachers worked with and for us to ensure that we would fulfill our intellectual destiny and by so doing uplift the race. My teachers were on a mission.

"For Black folks," hooks wrote, "teaching—educating—was fundamentally political because it was rooted in anti-racist struggle. Indeed, my all-black grade schools became locations where I experienced learning as revolution."

Later, hooks comments, "To be changed by ideas was pure pleasure."[1]

Her memories of her education fit beautifully into the history of Black educators in this country at the turn of the century. The dust of the Civil War had settled, sweeping away much of the Black progress of Reconstruction. Finally vested with the freedom and citizenship they had long fought for, the formerly enslaved were learning to grapple with life in the Jim Crow South. Slavery had been abolished, but a strict racial hierarchy remained, and stepping out of line was deadly.

Against this backdrop, Black leaders began the important work of educating the next generation of Black citizens. Prominent schools like M Street in Washington, DC, and The Haines Normal and Industrial Institute in Georgia cropped up to answer the call. They employed a rigorous curriculum steeped in the classics, and in many cases (like with Nannie Helen Burroughs National Training School for Women and Girls), they also offered trade education alongside their liberal arts curriculum.

For the first time in American history, Black leaders were having open conversations about how education should look for future generations. Black American teachers faced the unique task of teaching a generation that had shifted from a state of legislated illiteracy to one that included the opportunity for a thorough education.

And yet, even as these young Black students crowded into classrooms for the first time in history, they studied textbooks calculated to keep them in their place. Historian LaGarrett J. King writes:

> Central to this approach of racial subjugation were K-12 social studies textbooks written by White historians and educators who used history as a means to explore ideas of U.S. citizenship. It was common in these textbooks to underscore Black persons as inferior and second-class citizens. Early social studies textbooks emphasized that the "Black skin was a curse" (Woodson, 1933 p. 3) through narratives that purported that Black people were naturally "barbarians," "destitute of intelligence," or " having little humanity" (Brown, 2010; Elson, 1964; Foster, 1999). The racializations of Blackness were used as justifications for the paternalistic attitudes White citizens had towards African Americans.[2]

While finally empowered with the education so long withheld from them, Black children were taught by that very education that their Blackness was a curse. The shadow of white supremacy loomed large, even over educational institutions founded and upheld by the Black elite. And something needed to be done about it.

A New History

In 1890, attorney and teacher Edward A. Johnson wrote *A School History of the Negro Race in America from 1619 to 1890.* It was one of the first books of its kind—a history book written by a Black man for Black students. His preface begins:

> To the many thousand colored teachers in our country this book is dedicated. During my experience of eleven years as a teacher, I have often felt that the children of the race ought to study some work that would give them a little information on the many brave deeds and noble characters of their own race. I have often observed the sin of omission and commission on the part of white authors, most of whom seem to have written exclusively for white children, and studiously left out the many creditable deeds of the Negro. The general tone of most of the histories taught in our schools has been that of the inferiority of the Negro, whether actually said in so many words, or left to be implied from the highest laudation of the deeds of one race to the complete exclusion of those of the other.[3]

Johnson's message, put in modern terms: representation *matters*.

He wasn't the only one to realize the importance of representation. In 1912, Leila Amos Pendleton became what many consider the first Black female historian by writing her own textbook, *A Narrative of the Negro.* Her preface declares:

> In presenting this narrative, as a sort of "family story" to the colored children of America, it is my fervent hope that they may

hereby acquire such an earnest desire for greater information as shall compellingly lead them, in maturer years, to the many comprehensive and erudite volumes which have been written upon this subject.[4]

Later in the text, she expounds:

I came, therefore, to the irresistible conclusion in my mind that color is an accident affecting the surface of a man and having no more to do with his qualities than his clothes—that God had equally created an African in the image of his person and equally given him an immortal soul; and that an European had no pretext but his own cupidity, for impiously thrusting his fellow man from that rank in the creation which the Almighty had assigned him, and degrading him below the lot of the brute beasts that perish.[5]

Pendleton and Johnson were not alone in their quest to present Black children with accurate history that reflected their personhood. Gertrude Mossell, Laura Eliza Wilkes, Elizabeth Lindsay Davis, Delilah Beasley, Elizabeth Ross Haynes, Drusilla Dunjie Houston, Carter G. Woodson, and others used their time in the classroom as a catalyst for their passion for Black history. Aside from Woodson, none of these were historians in the academic sense, but they were laypeople who understood the power of Black history to solidify the Black personhood of their students in a time where that personhood was up for debate.

Representation mattered, they argued, not because Black Americans are *better* than their white counterparts, but because leaving out Black accomplishment and contribution tells a lie by omission. Black contribution has always been part of the American story.

The historical testimony serves to illuminate the personhood, the *imago Dei*, of these figures. The goal is not to paint the Black lives chronicled here as vested with more honor than their white counterparts but to remind the reader that they haven't been vested with less.

The routine disregard of Black image bearers in textbooks was not incidental—it was by design.

African American educators during the mid-nineteenth and early twentieth century understood that traditional textbooks "slander[ed] people of African descent, caus[ed] Black children to disidentify with their history and heritage, and distort[ed] their humanity." Therefore, African American educators during the mid-nineteenth and early twentieth century had a philosophical and political agenda in their approach to writing African American history textbooks. That purpose was to tenaciously challenge the prevailing ontological conceptions of African Americans. In other words, historical narratives helped frame the material conditions of African Americans in U.S. society. Textbooks became an important battleground for the fight for personhood status because African American educators believed that metaphorical and real acts of violence (physical, legal, and symbolic) began with school knowledge.[6]

After years of enslavement and dehumanization, Black American children were faced with an education system bent on trying to put them in their place. It's against this backdrop that Black historians took up the charge to uncover a history so long buried and obscured.

Education professor Chara Bohan shares that there was a concentrated effort on behalf of Southern educators to shift the historical narrative in the Confederacy's favor.

After the Civil War, from the 1870s through the 1910s, public schooling became more widespread in the South, and Confederate sympathizers wanted to ensure that their children received an "appropriate" education on Southern history and culture. To that end, Southern states developed statewide adoption policies for textbooks. This allowed the state textbook committees to control content by demanding changes or threatening to cancel book contracts unless the publishers acquiesced. Today, most of the states with statewide textbook adoption policies are still in the South.[7]

Put a different way: after Reconstruction, public education focused on white comfort and obscured the nation's history of white supremacy to the point of erasing Black American testimonies and experiences from their textbooks.

As Johnson wrote in the preface to his work, both the tearing down and omission of Black people from the narrative undermines Black personhood. If students never see figures who look like them in their textbook, they're inclined to think that it's not just the textbook but God himself omitting Black people.

And nothing could be further from the truth.

More than highlighting Black accomplishments, these historians felt it important to point out American shortcomings.

America holds a legacy of enslavement right alongside that of the enslaved advocating for their freedom; of crimes against Black bodies alongside a legacy of Black bodies resilient enough to demand their birthright by God's grace; of dainty, demure ideals of white femininity alongside the brutal sexual abuse of Black women; of bootstraps-tugging manhood amid the nepotism inherent in white supremacy and the disenfranchisement of generations of Black Americans.

America is complex, bearing its shame in tandem with its accomplishments, its pride right alongside its shortcomings.

By modern standards, Edward A. Johnson and Leila Amos Pendleton's history books are incredibly patriotic. They detail the contributions of Black citizens to the formation of America with unflinching honesty about the odds these citizens faced in their efforts to take part in the American dream.

Both wrote in the spirit of James Baldwin's famous quote from *Notes of a Native Son*:

I love America more than any other country in the world, and, exactly for this reason, I insist on the right to criticize her perpetually. I think all theories are suspect, that the finest principles may have to be modified, or may even be pulverized by the demands of life, and that one must find, therefore, one's own moral center and move through the world hoping that this center will guide one aright. I consider that I have many responsibilities, but none greater than this: to last, as Hemingway says, and get my work done.[8]

My moral center for this work is rooted in the Word of God. I realize these pages are not chock-full of extensive exegesis nor are the endnotes crawling with biblical commentaries, but my goal here is implicitly Christian: I have written of Black Christians who understood their rights came from the Word of God, defended those rights in word and deed, and forged citizenship for themselves in a country that claimed to be founded on them.

Because the Bible told them to do so.

Because the Word of God told them they were crowned with glory and honor, as the psalmist writes (Psalm 8:5), endowed with dignity by their Creator.

It's a simple aim, but so complex. During the cultural moment in which I pen these words, it feels more complex than ever. But my times are no more fraught than those of the men and women I have chronicled here. And I owe it to their legacy to continue speaking the truth in love.

When we tell the story of America, we *are* telling the story of something exceptional—and not always in a good way. But the image bearers who composed the story of America are more important than the often exaggerated lore of the country.

Students from every tribe, tongue, and nation deserve to know these stories—back then, now, and always.

This work is not born out of the hurts I experienced as a teacher but out of the hope that propels me to continue to teach. It is born out of the same aim of Pendleton and Johnson before me: to uphold Black humanity as brimming with identity, dignity, and significance that is rooted in humankind's status as human beings made in God's image.

I am no longer in the business of defending my humanity. I'm in the business of proclaiming it. And a long line of Black voices has stood before me proclaiming the same truth. We have been born of a country founded on the inherent dignity and rights of the white population that systemically denied the rights of the Black population, but this has not stopped us from walking in the truth of those rights or that dignity.

Proclaiming this dignity is a gospel issue, and as a believer, I am bound to proclaim it, whether in the pages of a book or in a classroom full of kids.

I hope to step back into the classroom someday. And whether my students look more like me than they used to, I hope I come armed not just with this resource but with a cacophony of voices that have been reclaiming the history so long obscured. I'm throwing my words into the ring, but there is so much more to be said by historians, sociologists, theologians, and others.

Here's one teacher's contribution to the story we must continue telling.

1

Give Me Liberty

Nat Turner and David Walker were both prophetic anti-slavery voices. One was born into slavery, one free—one used his pen to fight against slavery, and one took to the sword. But both men "struck a blow for liberty," in the words of nineteenth-century historian Leila Amos Pendleton.

Nat Turner and David Walker—two very different, very polarizing figures who fought for the dignity of the *imago Dei* very differently from some of the more "respectable" revolutionaries and abolitionists. They believed, as men like patriot-turned-activist James Forten did, that men and women were endowed with rights that should be protected and fought for. In Walker's case, that fight was idealistic—he wrote his *Appeal* in hopes that his thoughts would spur others to action. In Turner's case, his fight was very real and physical.

In his *Confessions*, Nat Turner tells the story of one of his very first visions. He was in the fields in the heat of the day, harvesting corn for his enslaver. He pulled back a corn husk and saw blood speckling the corn "like dew from heaven."

> For as the blood of Christ had been shed on this earth, and had ascended to heaven for the salvation of sinners, and was now returning to earth again in the form of dew—and as the leaves on the trees bore the impression of the figures I had seen in the heavens, it was plain to me that the Saviour was about to lay down the yoke he had borne for the sins of men, and the great day of judgment was at hand.[1]

In his *Appeal*, David Walker also takes a prophetic tone as he lambastes the corporate greed of American chattel slavery and calls on the enslaved to free themselves from the chains of bondage. He is one of the utilizers of the African American Jeremiad: a biblical exhortation that follows the example of the weeping prophet Jeremiah, who held Israel accountable for her disobedience to God.

If David Walker emulated the prophet Jeremiah in the tone and tenor of his own jeremiad—his *Appeal*—then Nat Turner emulated the prophet Ezekiel in his visions of the destruction of the slaveholders of Southampton, Virginia.

Turner's Sign

Nancy watched her little boy grow up in a world where she could not protect him.

Her own history had been lost to the waves of the Middle Passage, swallowed in a sea that claimed 1.5 million Black bodies on the treacherous voyage to American shores. Whether or not she shared her journey with her little boy, she did share what it had meant to be free—and what it had meant to have that freedom taken away from her.[2] She shared her dreams for her little boy—her visions of his future as a Moses to his people. And like Moses's mother Jochebed, who entrusted her son to the river rather than see him slaughtered at the hands of her own enslavers, Nancy entrusted her son's future to the Lord.

From an early age, the boy knew that he had been set apart for greater things. One of his earliest recollections was recounting a memory that could not have been his own—something that happened long before he'd been born.[3] As the years went on, everyone who knew him marked him as a remarkable child destined for great things. Given the rare gift of education, the boy became a man, buried himself in the Bible, and became known far and wide as a preacher with a powerful, prophetic voice.

He had read the words of Jeremiah the prophet, lamenting the injustices that cowed Israel in the face of foreign gods.

> Therefore I am full of the fury of the LORD; I am weary with holding in: I will pour it out upon the children abroad, and upon the assembly of young men together: for even the husband with the wife shall be taken, the aged with him that is full of days.
>
> And their houses shall be turned unto others, with their fields and wives together: for I will stretch out my hand upon the inhabitants of the land, saith the LORD.
>
> For from the least of them even unto the greatest of them every one is given to covetousness; and from the prophet even unto the priest every one dealeth falsely.
>
> They have healed also the hurt of the daughter of my people slightly, saying, Peace, peace; when there is no peace. (6:11–14)

His enslaved Virginia upbringing cried "Peace, peace"—the status quo was good enough; he had a kind enough master; he was well fed and taken care of; he was free to read the Bible and preach its truth to the enslaved . . .

But there was no peace.

One day, he was working in the fields when he heard a loud voice from heaven, which, as he related, said: "The Serpent was loosened, and Christ had laid down the yoke he had borne for the sins of men, and that I should take it on and fight against the Serpent, for the time was fast approaching when the first should be last and the last should be first."

He was to wait for a sign. And when the sign appeared, he was to be ready to act on every hope that his mother had poured into him.

Three years later, on February 13, 1831, late in the afternoon, the moon blotted out the light of the sun. As the man stared up at the solar eclipse, darkness covering the fields, "the seal was removed from his lips," and he was ready to communicate "the great work laid out for him to do."[4]

Nat Turner had received his sign.

Liberty or Death

Twenty-five years before Nat Turner was born in a slave cabin in Southampton, Virginia, another Virginian gave a speech that would change the course of American history.

America was on the verge of war.

Of this, Patrick Henry was sure.

And it was with the full force of this assurance that he stood at the Second Virginia Convention in 1775 at St. John's Church in Richmond, Virginia. The speech he gave would be an important marker on the road to the Revolutionary War, and Henry would go down in history as one of Virginia's most illustrious sons.

Henry "rose with an unearthly fire burning in his eye"[5] that belied the calm tone of his voice when he first began to speak. By the time he got to the words by which many know him, though, his voice was brimming with passion.

It is in vain, sir, to extenuate the matter. Gentlemen may cry, Peace, Peace—but there is no peace. The war is actually begun! The next gale that sweeps from the north will bring to our ears the clash of resounding arms! Our brethren are already in the field! Why stand we here idle? What is it that gentlemen wish? What would they have? Is life so dear, or peace so sweet, as to be purchased at the price of chains and slavery? Forbid it, Almighty God! I know not what course others may take; but as for me, give me liberty or give me death![6]

When Patrick spoke that final clause—*Give me liberty or give me death*—he beat his chest as though he were driving the dagger in himself.One onlooker reported that by the time he was done, "men looked beside themselves."[7]

The prestigious lawyer would go down in history as one of America's best orators, a fate that was likely sealed with this very speech. The willingness to die for freedom became a litmus test for the truest patriots—would they settle for a vacant, vapid peace, or would they fight until their dying breath for the real thing? Would they be lulled into calm by the chains of enslavement, or would they buck against those chains, even if it meant giving up their lives in the process?

Many know the answer that George Washington, Thomas Jefferson, and Patrick Henry gave. These men were clearly willing to risk it all for liberty. These three Virginians—the first president of the United States, the third president and drafter of the Declaration of Independence, and the eventual governor of Virginia—made history in the days following this dynamic oration by blazing a trail toward a country founded on the principles of the liberty that they were willing to die for.

And, to a man, they blazed this trail away from the "chains of slavery" while enslaving men, women, and children on their plantations back home.

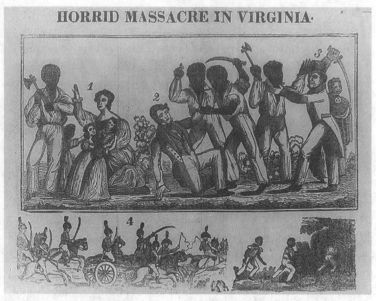

Nat Turner's Rebellion—the Southampton Insurrection, August 1831

Another Son of Virginia

Patrick Henry's home was not thirty miles away from where Nat Turner was born into slavery in 1800, just one year after Henry died. Young Nat's Virginia roots were just as deep as Washington's, Jefferson's, and Henry's before him. But instead of sprouting from the tree of free white American citizens who were encouraged to take up arms to defend their freedom, Turner was a descendant of the Black Americans who were routinely discouraged from doing the same.

From a young age, due to his mother's stories, Nat had a deep awareness that freedom was a birthright not meant to be confiscated.

Unlike many enslaved men, Nat was taught to read as a child, and he employed himself to reading the Bible. There, he saw the words that Patrick Henry quoted in the stirring conclusion of his speech:

26

They have healed also the hurt of the daughter of my people slightly, saying, Peace, peace; when there is no peace. (Jeremiah 6:14)

He would have read the bone-deep weariness of the weeping prophet as he cried out against the unrighteousness of Israel. And he would have seen the wrath that God was about to pour out against that unrighteousness: "Their houses shall be turned unto others, with their fields and wives together" because they have ignored the hurt they have caused (vv. 12, 14).

Turner saw the injustices that Jeremiah railed against writ large in his own enslavement. He watched children being ripped from their parents and sold away, never to be reunited. He saw enslaved wives taken from their husbands and taken into white men's beds. He saw harsh punishments inflicted on anyone who dared to stand up against the brutal status quo that defined American chattel slavery.

Nat Turner and Patrick Henry were both surrounded by people who told them to wait and see how things panned out. In Patrick Henry's case, by the time he rose to give his fateful speech, other delegates had cautioned against acting too rashly in rebellion to Great Britain; they had suggested that perhaps more peaceful measures could continue to advance the important conversation about American freedom. Perhaps, they said, everyone should wait.

Patrick Henry got up and declared that the time for talking was over.

And when Nat Turner saw that solar eclipse in February of 1831, he declared the same. "Is life so dear, or peace so sweet, as to be purchased at the price of chains and slavery. Forbid it, Almighty God!"

Forbid it indeed.

Speaking in Henry's Tradition

Before that solar eclipse, back when Nat Turner's budding rebellion was still hidden in his heart, David Walker was echoing Patrick Henry's warrior sentiment. Just a few years older than Turner, he had been born into freedom and made his home in the thriving Black middle class of Boston, Massachusetts. He made his living selling secondhand clothes, but writing is where he poured his passion.

Walker was the Boston correspondent for *Freedom's Journal*, America's first Black-owned newspaper. Though the *Journal* was short-lived, its enduring legacy remains in the writing of men like Nathaniel Paul, Samuel Eli Cornish, and David Walker himself. But Walker had another project burning in his chest: *An Appeal to the Colored Citizens of the World*.

A staunchly religious member of the African Methodist Episcopal Church, Walker aimed his appeal at the enslaved of the South. He referenced the revolution of which Henry partook, using his tract to lambaste the hypocrisy of the incomplete freedom that it purchased.

> I must observe to my brethren that at the close of the first Revolution in this country, with Great Britain, there were but thirteen States in the Union, now there are twenty-four, most of which are slave-holding States, and the whites are dragging us around in chains and in handcuffs, to their new States and Territories to work their mines and farms, to enrich them and their children—and millions of them believing firmly that we being a little darker than they, were made by our Creator to be an inheritance to them and their children for ever—the same as a parcel of *brutes*.[8]

Where Patrick Henry delivered his speech to the future powers that be of the nation in which Walker was born, Walker delivered his jeremiad to those that Henry overlooked in his own quest for freedom from tyranny.

And Walker aimed his pen directly at another son of Virginia in his text: Thomas Jefferson.

> Has Mr. Jefferson declared to the world, that we are inferior to the whites, both in the endowments of our bodies and our minds? It is indeed surprising, that a man of such great learning, combined with such excellent natural parts, should speak so of a set of men in chains.[9]

Doubtless, Walker had heard of Thomas Jefferson's book *Notes on the State of Virginia*, published in 1784, enjoying a "wide and impassioned readership."[10] In this work, as well as in his *Essay on the Anglo-Saxon Language*, Jefferson waxed eloquent on the inferiority of Africans. In an assumption that belied Walker's articulate future rebuttal of these prejudices, Jefferson wrote of the superior qualities of his "Saxon" readers:

> Add to these, flowing hair, a more elegant symmetry of form, their own judgment in favour of the whites, declared by their preference of them, as uniformly as is the preference of the Oranootan [orangutan] for the black women over those of his own species. The circumstance of superior beauty, is thought worthy attention in the propagation of our horses, dogs, and other domestic animals; why not in that of man?[11]

Notably, Jefferson and Henry had something in common besides their Virginian heritage, Revolutionary War mindsets, and the ownership of the enslaved: both felt that slavery was a contradiction to the freedom that they espoused. In Jefferson's case, he felt that slavery brutalized the enslaver; in other words, it was beneath the noble Saxon to barter in flesh.

In Henry's case, he wrote of slavery: "I will not, I cannot justify it. However culpable my conduct, I will so far pay my devoir to virtue as to own the excellence and rectitude of her precepts and lament my want of conformity to them."[12]

It was wrong—but it was convenient.

When Patrick Henry spoke about the convenience of slavery, America was responsible for anywhere from 4 to 6 percent of slavery fueled by the Middle Passage. By the year 1860, "two-thirds of all New World slaves lived in the American South."[13] This "convenience" amounted to four million enslaved souls at the dawn of the Civil War. This "convenience" was so lucrative that by the 1860s, there were more millionaires per capita in the Mississippi Valley than anywhere else in the United States.[14] It was so convenient that the slave trade generated more wealth

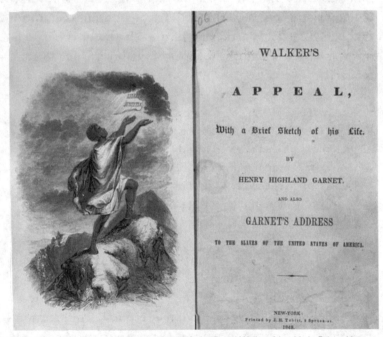

Walker's Appeal, with a Brief Sketch of His Life, by David Walker. New York: Printed by J. H. Tobitt, 1848, title page and frontispiece.

than the nation's banks, railroads, and factories combined. Is it any wonder that Frances Ellen Watkins Harper called American chattel slavery "a fearful alchemy by which this blood can be transformed into gold"?[15]

This convenience outpaced the rights of men like Nat Turner, their wives, and their children. These earnings were more important than the liberty of the enslaved in a nation that claimed to prize liberty above all else.

It was men like Nat Turner and David Walker—men who did not even merit American citizenship according to their nation's laws[16]—who held America accountable to her promises of liberty.

Was the Founding Fathers' patriotism outdone by an enslaved man?

Walker, Turner, and the *Imago Dei*

Walker understood that the principles of liberty that the Founding Fathers purported to believe flew directly in the face of the Black bodies that they enslaved. If man is endowed with inalienable rights by his Creator—and those rights are being systematically withheld from Black men—was Walker's manhood somehow in question?

Walker likely had Mr. Jefferson in mind when he declared:

Are we MEN!!—I ask you, O my brethren, are we MEN? Did our Creator make us to be slaves to dust and ashes like ourselves? Are they not dying worms as well as we? Have they not to make their appearance before the tribunal of Heaven, to answer for the deeds done in the body, as well as we? Have we any other Master but Jesus Christ alone? Is he not their Master as well as ours?—What right then, have we to obey and call any other Master, but Himself? How we could be so *submissive* to a gang of men, whom we cannot tell whether they are as good as ourselves or not, I never could conceive. However, this is shut

31

up with the Lord, and we cannot precisely tell—but I declare, we judge men by their works.[17]

Again and again in his *Appeal*, Walker returns to the fact that the oppression of slavery is occurring to people who have been "endowed by their Creator with certain unalienable Rights." But those rights were being infringed upon day in and day out by the brutality of slavery.

And David Walker had had enough.

Let no man of us budge one step, and let slave-holders come to beat us from our country. America is more our country, than it is the whites—we have enriched it with our *blood and tears*. The greatest riches in all America have arisen from our blood and tears:—and will they drive us from our property and homes, which we have earned with our *blood*? They must look sharp or this very thing will bring swift destruction upon them. The Americans have got so fat on our blood and groans, that they have almost forgotten the God of armies. But let them go on.[18]

If that last sentence sounds like a threat (a twenty-first-century Walker might have said, "Keep messing around and find out"), that's because it was. "If there is an *attempt* made by us," he wrote later, "kill or be killed."[19]

Walker's *Appeal* threw the Southern states into a frenzy. Between 1791 and 1804, the enslaved of Haiti had fought for their own liberation—and won. The newly minted United States of America quaked at the idea of the enslaved taking up arms against them; even as they had just taken up arms against the British to liberate themselves.

David Walker declared:

For although the destruction of the oppressors God may not effect by the oppressed, yet the Lord our God will bring other destruction upon them, for not infrequently will he cause them to rise up one against the other, to be split, divided, and to oppress each other, and sometimes to open hostilities with sword in hand.[20]

And that message was terrifying.

It was so terrifying, in fact, that a price was put on David Walker's head. His pamphlet was banned in several states, its dissemination yet another reason why slaveholders discouraged literacy among the enslaved. In their minds, Walker's radical ideas could stir up rebellion.

The Wrath of Image Bearers

The night of August 21, 1831, a white woman named Lavinia Francis crouched in the woods behind her home.

Her heart hammered in her chest as she watched the torches of the amassing groups of enslaved rebels that were pouring across the Southampton countryside. Her husband was dead. And even though she was eight months pregnant, she was sure to have met the same fate if one of the enslaved men had not taken pity on her. Red Nelson, who knew the family, had hidden Lavinia himself, urging her to stay quiet while his compatriots murdered every living member of every white household they came upon.

Men, women, and children.

Nat Turner killed ten-year-old Putnam Moore, his own legal owner, and had given orders that his followers were to kill *every white person they saw*. By the time they made it to Lavinia's home, they had already killed an infant.

At least on that first night, Nat was committed to showing no mercy.

Ezekiel 9:4–6 likely inspired this approach:

And the LORD said unto him, Go through the midst of the city, through the midst of Jerusalem, and set a mark upon the foreheads of the men that sigh and that cry for all the abominations that be done in the midst thereof.

And to the others he said in mine hearing, Go ye after him through the city, and smite: let not your eye spare, neither have ye pity:

Slay utterly old and young, both maids, and little children, and women: but come not near any man upon whom is the mark; and begin at my sanctuary. Then they began at the ancient men which were before the house.

When all was said and done, Turner and his men killed more than fifty white slaveholders in Southampton. Figures like Lavinia—who were spared by the kindness of one and not the intention of the many—would be held up as proof of the bloodlust and carnage of the rebels who would have surely killed her, had she not escaped.

Newspapers and government leaders placed the blame for this rebellion squarely on the Boston abolitionists, with the governor of Virginia calling out the "incendiary publications" of Walker and William Lloyd Garrison by name. *The Liberator*, a popular abolitionist paper, was termed "diabolical" and its editor an "instigator of human butchery." Boston's mayor was flooded with demands to silence Garrison and shut down his paper, some suggesting that he deserved the death penalty for inciting slaves to kill innocent whites.[21]

The theme of instigation would come up again and again in conversations about Nat Turner's rebellion. Surely, it was in teaching him to read that his first owner had made a critical error, some thought. Surely, thought others, it was in the revolutionary ideas bandied about by radical abolitionists.

It seemed to occur to very few that Nat Turner was, as David Walker had so eloquently written, a MAN. And as a man, he possessed those "unalienable Rights" that founded the very country that enslaved him. As a man, he could ask the very same question that David Walker asked: "What right then, have we to obey and call any other Master, but Himself?" As a man, he could cry out with the same thunderous voice that Patrick Henry had used, "*Give me liberty, or give me death.*"

It occurred to very few that, as an image bearer, Nat Turner could see the unchecked power of white enslavers and hearken to the Bible's harsh stance on the oppressor. Nat Turner could look at the white people of Southampton and note that not a single man, woman, or child sighed or cried "for all the abominations that be done in the midst thereof" (Ezekiel 9:4).

It occurred to very few that Nat Turner did not need David Walker's *Appeal* or William Lloyd Garrison's *The Liberator* or even the Declaration of the United States of America to tell him that he had inalienable rights; he found those rights in the Scriptures.

A Man Possessed

Nat Turner was thirty-one when he died. He was hanged, then skinned, then beheaded, to make an example of his rebellion. One imagines that Virginians were shocked that an enslaved man had walked into his enslaver's home in the middle of the night and killed his entire family.

But at least one Virginian might not have been surprised, had he lived to see the day.

In *Notes on the State of Virginia*, Jefferson wrote:

> It will probably be asked, Why not retain and incorporate the blacks into the state, and thus save the expence of supplying, by importation of white settlers, the vacancies they will leave? Deep rooted prejudices entertained by the whites; ten thousand recollections, by the blacks, of the injuries they have sustained . . .[22]

Elsewhere, Jefferson wrote, "But, as it is, we have the wolf by the ear, and we can neither hold him, nor safely let him go. Justice is in one scale, and self-preservation in the other."[23]

Note Jefferson's words: "Justice is in one scale, and self-preservation in the other." How long could "the corrupt, slave-holding, women-whipping, cradle-plundering, partial and hypocritical Christianity of this land"[24] expect to thrive without returning the "ten thousand recollections" of those injuries coming back onto white America's head?

Jefferson knew that a reckoning was coming.

And Nat Turner took his part in that reckoning, knowing that the cost would be his own life.

Give me liberty, the hatchet-wielding revolutionary's actions cried, *or give me death*.

Where Are the Heroes?

Nat Turner's violent quest for liberation turns many a modern reader's stomach. Understandably. Men, women, and children were slaughtered in his pursuit of justice. But the enslavement that led Turner to this violent uprising should turn a modern reader's stomach as much as it turned David Walker's. And if students of history are taught to believe that Patrick Henry was a son of America in his battle cry of liberty or death, then they must also recognize that Nat Turner is a son of America in *his* same battle cry.

One need not lift Turner up as a hero to understand his actions, considering the oppression of image bearers all around him. But if readers wish to lionize the Founding Fathers of yore, consistency might demand they not see Turner as a villain either.

If taxation without representation is enough inducement to incite a rebellion, then surely the selling of men, women, and children away from their families, the indiscriminate brutalization of their bodies, the barring of their voices from the very representation that their white countrymen fought for, is worth throwing some tea into the harbor.

Nat Turner isn't held up here as a figure to follow but rather as an illustration to heed. If liberty lovers take oppression seriously, then they must acknowledge that justice will not sleep forever. And when it awakes, woe to whoever is standing in the way.

In a 1969 interview with Dick Cavett, James Baldwin responded to a question about Black leaders who want to "burn it down, demolish it" ("it" being the American establishment). Baldwin famously answered:

> If any white man in the world says give me liberty or give me death, the entire white world applauds. When a black man says exactly the same thing—word for word—he is judged a criminal and treated like one, and everything possible is done to make an example of this bad nigger so there won't be any more like him.[25]

Baldwin posited that if white Americans truly understood the oppression that had beleaguered Black Americans for centuries, Nat Turner would be a hero.

Indeed, in the past, Black historians have been far less disapproving of Turner than their white counterparts. In *A Narrative of the Negro*, Leila Amos Pendleton compared him to Joan of Arc, and declared that "the time had come to strike a blow for the freedom of his people."[26] In *A School History of the Negro Race in America from 1619 to 1890*, Edward A. Johnson wrote:

> Nat kept up his courage to the last, and his neck in the noose, not a muscle quivered or groan was uttered. He was, undoubtedly, a wonderful character. Knowing as he did, the risk he ran, what an immense courage he must have had to undertake this bold adventure.[27]

Johnson records the lives of several others who "struck" for freedom: Avery Watkins, a Black preacher in North Carolina who was hung over a private conversation endorsing Turner's revolt; Madison Washington, an enslaved man who commandeered a cargo ship en route from New Orleans to Virginia and gained the freedom of all 135 souls on board; the *Amistad* captives who killed the captain of the ship that abducted them; Denmark Vesey, a pastor from the Caribbean who modeled a slave rebellion after the Haitian Revolution.

In fact, in 1739, before Patrick Henry even stood up to declare his now-famous ultimatum, over one hundred enslaved South Carolinians took part in the Stono Rebellion. Their banners declared "Liberty!" before the American soldiers made it their battle cry.

The enslaved did not need Patrick Henry to teach them how to advocate for liberty. They did not need Thomas Jefferson to declare their inalienable rights. They didn't even need David Walker to rally them to cry out against the chains that bound them.

Just like Jefferson, Washington, Henry, and others, enslaved men and women knew the truth of their dignity *because it was inherent in them* as people made in the image of God. Nat Turner's visions told him what so many enslaved image bearers already knew: that the just God of the universe created them and invested them with a value beyond that of chattel.

James Baldwin said it in 1969, but it was true in 1869, 1769, and 1619:[28] the desire to rebel and claim their freedom was not *new* for the enslaved; it was new for the enslavers.

In 1927, Blues singer Blind Willie Johnson recorded the song James Baldwin referenced in his answer to Cavett, "If I Had My Way I'd Tear This Building Down."

"Well, if I had my way / I had-a, a wicked mind / If I had-a, ah Lord, tear this building down."

The Negro spiritual had first been sung in the fields by the enslaved, their voices lifting to heaven in a rebellion that did not always culminate in hatchets, guns, or swords—a rebellion that didn't even always culminate in running to freedom. Sometimes, the rebellion came just in the singing—in the double meaning of the songs that rose toward heaven.

Sometimes, those songs gave secret messages of escape.

Sometimes, those songs gave secret messages of hope.

Sometimes, those songs gave secret messages of anger: *If I had my way, I'd tear it all down.*

In his poem "Warning," Langston Hughes wrote about the "docile" Negroes of the South and warned, "Beware the day they change their mind."

Their mind.

Because people made in the image of God were made to stand on equal footing alongside each other before the God of heaven. They were made to bow to him and him alone, not made to bow to and be cowed by the brutality of their fellow image bearers. And whether in a pamphlet, in a newspaper, in a speech, in the Bible, or from the voice of God himself booming from heaven, this knowledge cannot be hidden from image bearers forever.

2

A Double Victory

Nat Turner's brand of rebellion is rarely highlighted in history books, and when it does make an appearance, Turner is cast as a violent insurrectionist rather than an abolitionist hero.

Rarer still is the profile of a man like James Forten, who did not shake off the chains of slavery with the sword but with his pocketbook at his ornate dinner table.

Another branch of abolitionism—moral suasion—often attracted the coalition of abolitionists who did not believe in the full equality of those they wished to set free. Arguments for the *imago Dei* extended beyond the chains of slavery and into who should be considered worthy of American citizenship and liberty's birthrights.

The Library Company of Philadelphia

Thought to be James Forten

The Dinner Table

Nat Turner's blow for freedom sent shockwaves through the abolitionist community.

And it put abolitionist William Lloyd Garrison's life at risk.

Already known as a troublemaker, Garrison and his abolitionist newspaper, *The Liberator*, were a rallying point for abolitionists from Black orator Maria Stewart to white poet John Greenleaf Whittier. Unlike Turner and Walker, Garrison's brand of abolition was called "moral suasion," a nonviolent and apolitical approach to ending slavery. He relied on the inherent goodness in others to inform them of the wrongness of chattel slavery.

This did not mean Garrison held the matter of slavery lightly. Nor did it translate into his publication renouncing the actions of Turner.

On the contrary, in February of 1836, one of the newspaper's correspondents by the pen name "L" wrote:

Washington, who with our fathers purchased our freedom by blood and violence, are lauded as patterns of patriotism and Christianity. Nat Turner, and his associates, who endeavored to work out their own salvation from an oppression incomparably more grievous and unjust than our fathers endured, were treated as rebels, and murderous assassins, and were ruthlessly hung, or shot like wolves, and their memory is corrupt. (February 13, 1836)[1]

Of Nat Turner, Garrison later editorialized:

The name does not strike the ear so harmoniously as that of Washington, or Lafayette, or Hancock, or Warren; but the name is nothing. Is it not the power of all the slaveholders upon the earth to render odious the memory of that sable chieftain? "Resistance to tyrants is obedience to God," was our revolutionary motto. We acted upon the motto—what more did Nat Turner?[2]

Yet, for all his admiration of Turner, most of Garrison's abolitionist work occurred in the lectern, in print, or at a dinner table.

One table he regularly frequented was that of James Forten, the wealthy Black man whose donation helped to start *The Liberator*. Garrison, however, was neither the first nor the only kind of abolitionist to dine at Forten's table.

Robert Jefferson Breckinridge was born in 1800 of respectable American parents who could trace their heritage in the States back to 1728. Over the generations prior to his birth, the Breckinridge family journeyed to Kentucky, where they joined the ranks of slaveholders who populated the state. In addition to his Scotch Irish background, Robert also inherited a strong Presbyterian heritage. Though he strayed from his evangelical roots early on in life, he became a Presbyterian minister in Baltimore and a staunch abolitionist by middle age.

Known for its abundant hospitality, the Forten home had a revolving door for activists, philanthropists, and men of God. Breckinridge fit the bill.

Like Breckinridge, Forten could trace his lineage back to Philadelphia's harbors. In fact, Forten's American roots were lodged even deeper than the younger man's, his great-grandfather having arrived in Philadelphia in 1680.

Unlike the willing migration of the Breckinridge family, Forten's great-grandfather had been carried from West Africa in the hull of a ship. He was one of 12.5 million Black human beings turned cargo who were tossed over an endless expanse of sea toward a life of servitude in the Americas. An estimated 1.8 million of those travelers met their untimely death on those seas, owing to disease, failed revolts, or taking their own lives in the murky depths below.

But Forten's great-grandfather survived, though his name is lost to history. He arrived at the fledgling colony in Pennsylvania, a state that originally questioned whether it would adopt the legacy of slavery. And though it later became one of the first states to abolish the institution, the man died a slave.

If Robert Breckinridge had his way, the next generation of enslaved Americans would not die in bondage. He seemed the perfect houseguest for a staunch abolitionist like Forten, the picture of conscientious activism that the wealthy Black Pennsylvanian could get behind.

And, indeed, they agreed on many points.

Doubtless, Forten would have uttered a hearty *amen* to Breckinridge's assertion that

> you may take a man at his birth, and by an adequate system make him a slave—a brute—a demon. This is man's work. The light of reason and history and philosophy—the voice of nature and religion—the spirit of God himself proclaims that the being he created in his own image he must have created free.[3]

But Forten held his own opinions as to what was owed to Black men created in God's image in a country created in the image of liberty—and Breckinridge would have taken exception.

Because Forten believed that American citizenship should extend to everyone:

> We hold this truth to be self-evident that God created all men equal, and is one of the most prominent features in the Declaration of Independence and in that glorious fabrick of collected wisdom, our noble Constitution. This idea embraces the Indian and European, the Savage and the Saint, the Peruvian and the Laplander, the white Man and the African, and whatever measures are adopted subversive of this inestimable privilege, are in direct violation of the letter and spirit of our Constitution, and become subject to the animadversion of all, particularly those who are deeply interested in the measure.[4]

Forten wrote these words in his *Letters from a Man of Colour* in 1813 after hearing of the passage of a bill aimed at limiting the immigration of free Black people into Pennsylvania. In this series of five anonymous letters, Forten argued for the rights of Black Americans, rooting his argument in the Declaration of Independence and the Constitution.

And on this finer point—that Black men created in God's image were equally deserving of rights as citizens of America—Breckinridge couldn't agree.

Who Are Citizens?

In Breckinridge's estimation, James Forten, though hospitable and well-spoken—was an anomaly, one he did not want to see become commonplace.

In the July 1833 edition of the *Biblical Repertory*, years before he sat at James Forten's dinner table, Breckinridge spoke out about free Black men like his host:

> First, then, as to the free people of colour. We hazard nothing in asserting that the subsisting relations between this class of persons and the community cannot remain permanently as they are. In the year 1790 there were sixty-three whites to every single free coloured person in this nation: in 1830, there were only thirty-five to one. A similar rate of approximation for about two centuries and a half would make the free coloured persons equal to the whites, without taking slaves at all into the account. Neither the safety of the State nor the resources of any community would endure within its bosom such a nation of idle, profligate, and ignorant persons.

Breckinridge agreed with Forten that the treatment of these "idle, profligate, and ignorant" "free people of colour" was unacceptable given the promises set forth in the Declaration of Independence:

> But that it is really most degraded, destitute, pitiable, and full of bitterness, no man who will use his senses can for one moment

doubt. And whatever their condition, that it has been brought upon them, chiefly if not entirely by our own policy and social state, is just as undeniable. They are victims to our fathers and to us; how, we pause not to ask. But they are victims: and every sentiment of religion impels us to regard their case with an eye of pity.[5]

But in Breckinridge's mind, the cure for the degradation foisted upon Black people in America wasn't full and equal citizenship. *May it never be!* Rather, Breckinridge embraced another solution: full-scale deportation of all Black people in America back to their native land—in this case, the colony of Liberia.

As it turns out, Breckinridge found himself in good company. He was a member of the American Colonization Society, which had been founded in 1816 with the stated purpose of helping Black people in America emigrate to Africa. Its founder, another Presbyterian minister named Robert Finley, felt Black people were "unfavorable" to the "industry and morals" of white Americans, and that their removal would cease interracial marriage and other intermingling.[6]

Finley's brother-in-law, Elias B. Caldwell, was a Supreme Court clerk. Together, Finley, Caldwell, and Francis Scott Key (of "Star-Spangled Banner" fame) canvassed to support their new venture. They convinced a few slaveholders to free their property, promising liberty to the enslaved under the condition that they leave the country once they were set free.

Opinions and motives surrounding colonization varied. Some white Americans saw an opportunity to rid themselves of Black freedmen, while others remained intent on creating free and thriving societies for Black people who wanted to emigrate. There were also colonization efforts altogether separate from the American Colonization Society, such as the work of Paul Cuffee, a Black ship captain and even wealthier friend of James Forten.

Robert Breckinridge fell into the former category. Unlike Finley, he was less worried about intermarriage (he looked favorably on "mulattoes," seeing them as closer to white than their "unmixed" counterparts[7]) than the presence of free Black people of a certain complexion.

Free Black people like James Forten.

This is the part of the Venn diagram where the overlap appeared between a man like Breckinridge (who considered himself a "benevolent slaveholder") and the committed slaveholders of the South: free Blacks were a threat.

For slaveholders, the existence of free Black people was something that could contribute to more Turner-style uprisings. If the enslaved population couldn't be useful in labor, many slaveholders believed they were better off being sent to Africa.

Breckinridge's brethren at the American Colonization Society had much to say about their desire to see Black Americans deported.

> If they must remain in their present situation, keep them in the lowest state of degradation and ignorance. The nearer you bring them to the brutes, the better chance do you give them of possessing their apathy.
>
> —Elias B. Caldwell

> What right, I demand, have the children of Africa to an homestead in the white man's country? . . . The ready answer is, because the African race is despised . . . that the descendants of Ham are inherently and naturally inferior to ourselves and others, the children of Shem and Japheth.
>
> —Washington Parke Curtis

> No matter how great their industry, or how abundant their wealth—no matter what their attainments in literature, science or the arts—they can never, no never be raised to a footing of equality.
>
> —Cyrus Edwards[8]

It's as though they were speaking directly to James Forten. It did not matter that Forten's family had been in America even longer than many of the white members of the American Colonization Society. It did not matter that he was significantly wealthier than many of the men who pontificated about his unworthiness to citizenship. It didn't even matter that he raised accomplished daughters and impressive sons or that his wife had entertained literal princes in her parlor.

To many white Americans, the Fortens were merely a Black family. At best, they were an exception to the inferiority that Caldwell, Curtis, and Edwards assumed. At worse, they were anomalies who could just as easily have been as useful in slavery.

An American Heritage

Thomas Forten raised his young son with a vast knowledge of ships, which was appropriate given Philadelphia's booming shipping industry. But James's appreciation for ships might have gone deeper than the sail-making trade his father passed along to him. For James, along with his siblings, ships were not just how his father put food on the table or how he amassed a fortune. Ships held a meaning far deeper than a paycheck.

While many Americans had grown accustomed to generational slavery during James's time, his great-grandfather was born into a country just starting to shape its understanding of the institution that would build a nation.

James's great-grandfather was likely alive when Virginia enacted the law of hereditary slavery in 1662, solidifying the passing down of race-based chattel slavery from mothers to their children for centuries. His own son, also nameless in modern American memory, would have inherited his enslaved mother's status.

Perhaps if James's family line had sprouted up in Virginia, his story would have been different. His family line might have been lost to the annals of history like so many other Black family lines of the period, erased by an institution that valued Black bodies as property rather than posterity; a white man's inheritance and not an inheritance in and of itself.

But the Forten family tree sprouted in Pennsylvania where James's grandfather was allowed to earn his own money on the docks and purchase his own freedom. He married a free woman and passed that freedom on to his descendants.

A ship brought James's great-grandfather to America and relegated him to a life of bondage.

Ships also bought James's grandfather his freedom and gifted his descendants that legacy.

James's father, Thomas, is the first ancestor modern students can name. As a young Black man in Philadelphia, he was free to work for an honest wage, which he did for a white sailmaker named Robert Bridges. Every day, he passed by the two Black men enslaved to Robert Bridges and watched several white indentured servants conduct his employer's business for no pay.

Perhaps Thomas's father had instilled in him the knowledge that ships could mean both enslavement *and* freedom for the Black men at Philadelphia's harbors. Thomas worked them to make a free life for himself. He married a good woman, provided for his family, and lived comfortably without fear.

When James was born in 1766, Thomas held that little boy and set his mind on what key the ships could pass to the next generation. As he watched his son grow from mewling infant to daredevil toddler to curious little boy, Thomas understood his own father in ways he never had before.

Early on, Thomas taught James how to fashion the key to his future. The little boy was barely out of diapers when Thomas brought him to the sail-making loft for the first time. James watched his father wield needle and thread on cloth sails so massive they had to be hoisted in through the loft windows instead of carried up the narrow steps.

The next year, James started sweeping the floor for scraps of fabric and thread, sorting what could be reused and what would be thrown away. He scrambled around with the gigantic West Indian cockroaches that tumbled out of the Caribbean ships docked in the Delaware River's harbor.

The year after that, James started working with the needle and thread. Unlike the small tools his mother used for mending, this needle was big enough to slice through the canvas of a sturdy sail, the thread coarse enough not to snap as he worked. Thomas stood over his son with a watchful eye, delighting in his progress. And when Robert Bridges took an interest in his young son, Thomas knew he'd fashioned the key to James's future.

The boy was only six years old when Thomas first became ill. James watched as his father's savings dried up. He watched as his mother sat up late at night, trying to calculate how to stretch the meager earnings Thomas was able to gather through a little work from home.

He watched as his strong, hardworking father gave in to frailty—as he eventually died, leaving James's widowed mother to care for James and his sister.

James's journey to sail-making apprenticeship would not be a linear one. He participated in the Revolutionary War, traveled to England, and continued his education, but when he finally settled back home in Philadelphia as a young man, Bridges received him. The older man taught James everything he knew, and when Bridges was ready to retire, he arranged a loan for James to buy his business from him.

Within three years, the business belonged to James, who turned those sails into the key to his fortune.

But ships would be more than the key to James's wealth. They would become the key to freedom. He spent half of his fortune liberating the enslaved, pouring as much money as he could into anti-slavery activism.

But his sailmaking and activism didn't stop with his family. He brokered the freedom of hundreds of Black Americans fighting for their birthright. What Thomas's papa did for young Thomas, James did for so many more.

Thomas's grandfather had been brought to America with the billowing sails of a slave ship. And Thomas's son, James, would become one of the wealthiest Black men in America because of the billowing sails in Philadelphia's harbors.

James Forten's story is the rags-to-riches stuff that the American dream is made of.

He was born long before Emma Lazarus's poem adorned the as-yet-uncrafted Statue of Liberty, heralding:

> Give me your tired, your poor,
> Your huddled masses yearning to breathe free,
> The wretched refuse of your teeming shore.
> Send these, the homeless, tempest-tost to me,
> I lift my lamp beside the golden door!

Forten died just thirty years before the legendary Gilded Age produced far wealthier rags-to-riches icons like Andrew Carnegie and Cornelius Vanderbilt, infusing American mythology with the idea that anyone from anywhere could come to America and make it big in business.

James Forten appears to be their forerunner.

Is there a rags-to-riches story more impressive than a family going from slave ship to shipping magnate in two short generations?

Not only was Forten a shrewd businessman, he was also a Revolutionary War veteran. At just fourteen, Forten used his familiarity with ships to join American privateer *Royal Louis*. When the HMS *Amphion* overtook *Royal Louis*, Forten became a prisoner of war. The conditions of American POWs aboard British ships were notoriously harrowing, but the captain of

Amphion had two young sons, and James became their favored playmate. This relationship likely saved Forten's life, and the teen was traded for British POWs shortly after his capture, returning him to freedom.

As an adult, Forten would hearken back to his privateer days as proof of his sterling record of patriotism. And he would understand his own American heritage as proof of his citizenship in a country that often wished to deny it. As a young man, Forten joined the effort to defend the country that he loved, and that country's values, he argued, saw him as an equal to the white men who surrounded him.

A Lesson for Breckinridge

By the time James Forten and Robert Breckinridge sat down to dinner together, Forten had made his opinion on the matter of colonization widely known. In 1817, he presided over a meeting of more than three thousand free men of color in the first African Methodist Episcopal Church in Philadelphia, Mother Bethel, which would become a bastion of abolition and civil rights for years to come, and this inaugural meeting would stand as a flash point. The pastor, Richard Allen, founder of the AME Church, stood alongside Forten as they registered together the unanimous objections of the crowd gathered before them. The two men led the charge in forming a resolution against colonization.

> Whereas our ancestors (not of choice) were the first successful cultivators of the wilds of America, we their descendants feel ourselves entitled to participate in the blessings of her luxuriant soil, which our blood and sweat manured. . . . having a tendency to banish us from her bosom, would not only be cruel, but in direct violation of those principles, which have been the boast of this republic. Resolved, That we view with deep abhorrence the

unmerited stigma attempted to be cast upon the . . . people of color, by the promoters of this measure. . . . Resolved, That we never will separate ourselves voluntarily from the slave population in this country.[9]

Forten's participation occurred twenty years before Robert Breckinridge sat at his table. He was fourteen years Breckinridge's elder, and his American lineage outspanned the man's by more than triple that. He was likely wealthier than Breckinridge and more established as a forward Northern thinker than his Kentucky counterpart.

And yet, even though Breckinridge gave lip service to James Forten and his family being made in the image of God, the younger man saw that image as having limitations.

Now that Forten's and Breckinridge's positions have been established and what each has at stake, let's turn back to their fateful dinner. It was only a couple of years after Nat Turner's 1831 rebellion, and Forten and Breckinridge were discussing a situation in Haiti. Reaching an impasse, Forten produced a letter from a Haitian contact and passed it to Breckinridge to prove his point. Breckinridge balked, confessing he did not speak French.

Forten summoned his daughter Margaretta, who would have been just a few years younger than Robert and unmarried, to translate the letter.

The oldest of his daughters, Margaretta was a school founder and headmistress who wrote for William Lloyd Garrison's *The Liberator*, a paper her father helped fund. She was an antislavery activist in her own right, having started the Philadelphia Female Anti-Slavery Society with her mother, sisters, and sister-in-law. She even had a hand in drawing up the society's constitution.

If anyone stood in contrast to Breckinridge's low opinion of Black freedmen, it was the distinguished Forten family.

Doubtless aware of his prejudice, they hosted him with the dignity for which they were known in Philadelphia. When he left, they may have even thought he learned a thing or two about his assumptions concerning the inferiority of their race.

In March of 1839, however, the *Herald of Freedom* reported on the anecdote:

> [A]t tea [Breckinridge] disputed him [James Forten] on some point of Haitian politics. To sustain his position, Mr. F. called on his daughter for a document he had received from a correspondent at St. Domingo. It was produced and handed to Mr. B. It was in French, and Mr. B. not being acquainted with that language, Mr. F. directed his daughter to read it to him. She did. Mr. Breckenridge expressed surprise at her acquaintance with the French—but going into a Colonization meeting in the city after tea, he argued the *natural incapacity* and *inferiority* of the colored people as a reason why they should be sent to Africa.[10]

Breckinridge witnessed Margaretta's intelligence, experienced James's hospitality, and agreed with their anti-slavery cause. And yet he still concluded a natural inferiority about his hosts, accompanied by a desire for America to be rid of people like them.

To quote Cyrus Edwards of the American Colonization Society again: *"No matter how great their industry, or how abundant their wealth—no matter what their attainments in literature, science or the arts—they can never, no never be raised to a footing of equality."*

Artwork of Margaretta Forten

54

Embittered Feelings

It's unclear if Margaretta found out about Breckinridge's slight before or after it was reported in *Herald of Freedom* (more on that later). However, her younger sister Sarah did share her thoughts about the slights that she and her family often endured because of the color of their skin. In a letter to one of the Grimké sisters, she wrote:

> In reply to your question—of the "effect of Prejudice" on myself, I must acknowledge that it has often embittered my feelings. I am peculiarly sensitive on this point. It has often engendered feelings of discontent and mortification when I saw that many were preferred before me, who by education, birth, or worldly circumstances were no better than myself, THEIR sole claim depending on being *White*. I am striving to live above such heart burnings.[11]

Sarah wasn't the only Forten who communicated a keen awareness of the prejudice directed at her family. The most direct insult to James in the matter of Margaretta and Breckinridge came not from the American Colonization Society member but from Nathaniel P. Rogers, the editor of *Herald of Freedom* himself.

Forten realized he had been receiving the *Herald* for a year without a bill. He sent along five dollars, as well as a thank-you note written with his usual gentility. Rogers was so thrilled by the thank-you note that he published it in the *Herald* along with the following description:

> We publish the above letter because, first, we want among our readers the benefit of its good opinion of the Herald . . . further, that our brethren many of whom have heard of the noble man may see a letter from the hand of James Forten—further, in slight token of our high respect, and perhaps not the last, that

our generous minded pro-slavery sneerers (who can read) may see how "N[—]." write—for JAMES FORTEN OF PHILA-DELPHIA IS A "N[—]."[12]

Rogers wanted so desperately to make a point to the pro-slavery sect that he insulted one of the wealthiest benefactors of his paper. Feeling every bit of the slight, Forten confronted Rogers:

> He and his family felt about their every utterance, their every move, being commented upon. Their privacy was constantly being violated, and they heartily disliked the "well meant, though injudicious, and sometimes really impolite notice which is taken, if any of us happen to do, or say any thing like other people." After all, "if we have the same opportunity's of education, and improvement, what is there to prevent our being just like others, who have these advantages?"[13]

Forten wanted to be seen as an American gentleman, no more and no less, but everywhere he turned, he was taken for so much less. Yet even in his frustration, he displayed restraint and gentility. Despite his wealth, business savvy, and social standing, he knew he risked his social capital every time he went head-to-head with men like Breckinridge. He also knew he was seen as the exception to many "rules" about who Black men were allowed to be in polite society.

In 1842, geologist Sir Charles Lyell of Scotland remarked upon the hundreds of people who showed up to watch Forten's funeral procession. He saw people of different ethnicities and classes gather to bid a fond farewell to the shipping magnate. Lyell was confused to find that, though Forten was highly respected, "his sons had been refused a hearing at a public meeting . . . to speak on some subject connected with trade"[14] because of the color of their skin.

Forten scholar Julie Winch writes:

Being "an exception to his race" was hardly a comfortable role for James Forten. It meant that, although he could "rise in the world," there were certain bounds he and his children could not overstep. But what were those bounds? How did Forten try to negotiate his way around them? When was he successful, and when did the forces of racial proscription prove too powerful even for someone of his tact and ingenuity?[15]

Forten was constantly navigating what it meant to be seen as an exception to the general rule of Black inferiority. His business prowess, though undeniable, was considered rare. Few of his contemporaries believed, if given the same opportunities, other Black men would rise to Forten's level.

An Exception to the Rule

Still, Forten continued to blaze trails and advocate for the rights of *all* Black men. Not just those deemed as exceptional.

Where David Walker used his pen like a lightning rod and Nat Turner took up arms to secure his freedom, James Forten let his money and his character talk for him. In addition to *The Liberator*, his funds founded *Freedom's Journal* and bankrolled other abolitionist causes. He even supported Paul Cuffe's program to help Black Americans emigrate to Sierra Leone.

Were Breckinridge devoted to a cause Forten could support, Forten would have gladly contributed funds to such a venture. And yet, despite being a wealthy benefactor and a gentleman, Forten was seen as less, even by some of his abolitionist peers.

Even by people who understood he was made in the image of God.

Breckinridge might have understood, as he said, "the spirit of God himself proclaims that the being he created in his own image he must have created free," but he did not understand that being made in the image of God conferred *dignity* and *equality* to image bearers.

Breckinridge saw Forten as made in God's image . . . but not worthy of respect. He saw Forten as deserving of freedom, but not citizenship. Forten, who had been a prisoner of war in the fight for America's independence at the tender age of fourteen, was not seen as equal to a man who had been born in a free country, in part, because of Forten's efforts.

As Black soldiers entered the conflict of World War II, James G. Johnson wrote:

Being an American of dark complexion and some 26 years, these questions flashed through my mind: "Should I sacrifice my life to live half American?" "Will things be better for the next generation in the peace to follow?" "Would it be demanding too much to demand full citizenship rights in exchange for the sacrificing of my life?" Is the kind of America I know worth defending? . . . Will Colored Americans suffer still the indignities that have been heaped upon them in the past?

The V for victory sign is being displayed prominently in all so-called democratic countries which are fighting for victory over aggression, slavery, and tyranny. Let we colored Americans adopt the double VV for a double victory the first V for victory over our enemies from without, the second V for victory over our enemies within.[16]

This double victory would not be a reality for many years to come. In fact, in 1946 Isaac Woodard, a Black army sergeant on his way home to South Carolina, was pulled from a bus after arguing with the driver. Police officers beat him so severely that he was blinded for the rest of his life.

He later recalled, "The policeman asked me, 'was I discharged?' and when I said, 'yes,' that's when he started beating me with a billy near across the top of my head."[17]

No doubt, Breckinridge would point to this tragedy as proof that Black and white Americans simply weren't meant to co-exist in this country, and further, that "American" could only be properly applied to the latter category of men. Never mind the fact that Americans like James Forten and Isaac Woodard had fought and sacrificed to make America a reality.

When Isaac Woodard argued with the bus driver before his fateful altercation with police, he said something that would have resonated with James Forten, Nat Turner, and David Walker: "I'm a man just like you."

Those simple words represented a truth that Breckinridge, for all his abolitionist notions, ultimately denied. He didn't consider James Forten a man "just like him." He believed him a different kind of being. Made in God's image, yes, but somehow lesser. Made to be free, yes, but a different *kind* of freedom than his own.

Forten knew this when he invited Breckinridge to his dinner table.

He fought against the prejudices of Breckinridge and others with a grace different from his hatchet-wielding contemporary Nat Turner. But both fought to be recognized, not just as men, but as equals—as Americans. They warred on two different fronts, in the heat of two different battles, but their struggle would be recognized as men made in the image of God and endowed with rights by their Creator.

"I'm a man, just like you," David Walker said repeatedly in his *Appeal*.

"I'm a man, just like you," James Forten wrote in his *Letters from a Man of Colour*.

Forten's daughters would join the chorus with their own verse: "We are women just like you."

3

The Double Curse

As a young girl, Margaretta Forten translated a French letter for abolitionist Robert J. Breckinridge. Her abilities impressed him so much that he was awed in the moment. They also impressed him so little that, within hours, he was still arguing the inferiority of Black people.

Margaretta Forten represents an oft-overlooked story in the landscape of abolition (at least for laypeople): the free Black woman. They juggled their aspirations and responsibilities in a world of strict, Victorian ideals of femininity from which they were often barred. They did not enjoy the same freedom as men. Instead, they occupied a no-man's-land where they were disrespected for being Black women. They had none of the security offered by white, middle-class femininity, but all the burdens. They had none of the mobility, however limited, afforded to free Black males, but all the hardships.

Robert Purvis called it the "double curse," and in this chapter, we'll discuss how these women navigated it.

In 1833, a young woman mounted the stage at a benefit for the education of the formerly enslaved. Though her name has been lost to history, her words live on in an issue of *The Liberator*. Attributed simply to "a young lady of color," the speech is succinct, yet powerful. As it crescendos, the young lady makes a familiar claim:

> Hear the cries of the tender mother, when torn asunder from her beloved infant and husband, and sold to a cruel master, and perhaps never more to meet them on earth. Hear her crying in the agonies of despair, "Am I not a woman and a sister?" I would ask the question, is she not? Certainly, she is.[1]

The image of the slave mother was a common refrain for those assembled in the presence of this young, passionate abolitionist. In 1831, Sarah Forten, daughter of James and sister of Margaretta, published a poem about a child encouraging her enslaved mother with the truth that "God will be our guard."[2] Frances Ellen Watkins Harper would use the shocking imagery of a slave mother in her poem "The Slave Mother" twenty years later, asking her readers, "Heard you that shriek?" of a grieving mother.

The image was such a mainstay of abolitionist rhetoric that James Redpath, an abolitionist from Scotland, would rely heavily on it in his book *The Roving Editor*, where he recorded his interactions with the enslaved of the South.

> "Have any of your children been sold?" I inquired.
>
> "Yes," she said, sobbing, the tears beginning to trinkle down her furrowed cheeks, "three on 'em. Two boys were sold down South—I don't know where they is; and my oldest son was sold to Texas three years since. There was talk about him coming back, but it's bin talked about too-oo-oo"—her sobs interrupted her speech for a few seconds—"too-oo-oo long to be true, I's afeerd."

Her maternal affections were strongly moved; I knew she would answer any questions now.

"It must have been very hard with you to part with your boys; almost as hard as when your other children died?" I said.

"Almost, massa?" she rejoined, "far wuss. When they're dead, it seems as if we knowed they wus gone; but when they're sold down South—ah!—ah!—massa"—

She did not finish the sentence in articulate words, but the tears that raced down her wrinkled face, the sighs that heaved her bereaved maternal breast, concluded it more eloquently than her tongue could have done. "It almost broke my heart, massa," she said, "but we cannot complain—*we's only slaves.*"

The enslaved woman he spoke to was sixty-two when she related this experience to him in 1854. Redpath recorded her story with several asides to his intended audience for the work: "my fair sisters of the North," "ladies, lovely, of the North."

He hoped the "lovely ladies of the North" would not be able to turn a blind eye to the suffering of the slave mothers of the South. He saw the injustice endured by slave mothers as a particularly egregious slight, writing that he wished he could punish the "Southern pro-slavery divines in the world to come."[3]

Collection of the Smithsonian National Museum of African American History and Culture

"Am I not a woman and a sister?"

The logo of the Ladies' Department of *The Liberator*, where Sarah Forten and others had their words published, displayed a slave woman on bended knees, chained hands supplicating heaven, with the words above her head asking: "Am I not a woman and a sister?"

These women knew all too well America's complicated legacy of answering that question.

A Virtuous Woman

During the nineteenth century, the Cult of True Womanhood was in full effect. The tenets of this social movement, centered around the iron-clad morals and weeping frailty of the ideal woman, were simple enough:

> The attributes of True Womanhood, by which a woman judged herself and was judged by her husband, her neighbors and society could be divided into four cardinal virtues—piety, purity, submissiveness and domesticity. Put them all together and they spelled mother, daughter, sister, wife-woman. Without them, no matter whether there was fame, achievement or wealth, all was ashes. With them she was promised happiness and power.

Historian Barbara Welter goes on to state, "Religion or piety was the core of woman's virtue, the source of her strength."[4] The women of this movement (also called True Womanhood) were taught that feminine grace's truest power was in the unhampered virtue of young women. Thus, women found their greatest callings primarily as wives and mothers, and secondarily as sympathetic sisters in arms.

They were expected to possess a strong, undaunted moral fiber wrapped in the tender, fragile shell of Victorian beauty standards. Frailty was in such high demand that tuberculosis became quite the fashionable disease. In her book *Consumptive Chic*, historian Carolyn A. Day describes the way standards of beauty and symptoms of sickness became intertwined:

> The symptoms were not only compatible with popular ideals of beauty, but the dominant presentation of tuberculosis was that of a disease characterized by attractive aesthetics. This was made possible, in part, by a congruence of factors including

disease mortality, advances in the approach to illness, and the influence of the key social movements of the era. The cultural expectations that developed for tuberculosis, as a result of these broader changes, were articulated in medical treatises, literature, poetry, and the works that sought to define fashion and the female role. All of these provided examples that connected the hallmarks of beauty with the symptoms of tuberculosis, and as such, reveal a shared consciousness that the disease was aesthetically pleasing.

Day also highlights the influence of the Cult of True Womanhood:

> The gender-based boundaries tended to highlight the independent healthy male body as a central component of the working world, and as a fundamental attribute of respectable masculinity. On the other hand, respectable femininity was allied to physical frailty, domesticity, and dependence.[5]

If women are meant to be pious and virtuous, shouldn't a system perpetuating their rape and dishonor be abhorred? If women are meant to be weak and demurring, shouldn't a system that has them working in the fields alongside men be thrown aside? If women are meant to be kept tender and protected, shouldn't a system reliant upon their *lack* of protection and the stripping away of their tenderness be reviled?

Well, yes.

But only if people view those women as the same *type* of women as their white counterparts.

If the imagery of white Christian motherhood was one of modesty, propriety, and virginity, most Black enslaved women failed to fit the bill. Contrast the enslaved woman with her enslaver's white wife: in the Victorian era, women were focused on ideals of modesty and decorum.

When it is remembered, that modesty was made for woman, and woman was made for modesty, we must say, nothing ornaments and embellishes a female more than modest apparel and a prudent demeanour, and vice versa, with immodesty and imprudence.[6]

Victorian women lived by a strict dress code. Not only were they to clothe themselves with modesty from their tightly laced corsets to their embroidered slippers, they also had to know what fabrics, accessories, and hairstyles to wear for each occasion. Their daily encounters were monitored by unwavering rules of decorum.

Of course, this was not so with the enslaved women of the South.

The dehumanization and hypersexualization of black women was so systemic that it was woven into the very fabric of society; their optimal breeding times were the topic of dinner conversations, and they were sold in market in little to no clothing as potential buyers prodded and poked their frequently pregnant bellies to assess their "breeding" potential. Often forced to dress in rags, with legs, arms, and sometimes chest showing, they provided a deliberately marked contrast to the fully and heavily clothed white women, which, as bell hooks has noted, both reinforced their supposed innate lack of chastity and morality, and exposed them to yet more abuse: "the nakedness of the female slave served as a constant reminder of her sexual vulnerability."[7]

But even when Black women donned themselves in the same clothing as their white counterparts, they were met with mockery and disdain. In 1829, William Simpson commissioned a series of eleven prints meant to mock the up-and-coming middle class of Philadelphia—primarily the free Black people (like the Fortens) who were carving out their place in society.

The imagery depicts Black women as "overdressed, overweight, poorly educated, childish social climbers."[8] The dialogue is cast in mocking dialect and shows Black Philadelphians as inept at wielding the freedom so many of their peers craved.

In one image, a Black woman named "Angelica" sits and reads a "lub letter" from a man enthralled with her:

My Fairest Angelica

Dy Slender form and Classic Features hab made sich an impression on my poor heart dat I cannot tink ob anything else. Indeed I must be de Blackest of Villains if I could see sich lubliness widout feeling its Influence as de Song says.—"Eyes ob fire lips ob Dew / Cheeks dat shame the roses hue"

I remain your Adorable Lubber

Augustus Octavio Whiteman.[9]

THE LUB LETTER.

The joke for contemporary readers was clear: this Black woman, literally rendered in coal-black pencil, with clownishly big feet bursting the seams of her slippers and ghoulish teeth poking from oversized lips, is meant to be laughable. The idea that any man would find her lovely, more laughable still.

Such mocking imagery wasn't reserved for enslaved women alone. In one corner of society, the virtuous white woman thrived, shielded from the male gaze by yards of fabric and miles of social decorum. In the other corner sat the Black woman, who, whether enslaved or free, was judged based on how the most wretched members of her race were treated on the auction blocks down South.

The picture of the Black woman, then, her poignant question of womanhood and sisterhood, was not rhetorical. These women cried out for their womanhood to be affirmed in a society hell-bent on erasing all but the reproductive abilities associated with femininity.

Changing the Narrative

Elizabeth Key Grinstead became the first Black woman in the colonies to successfully sue for her freedom in 1656. Born to a white planter and a Black woman, she filed her freedom suit as a grown woman, claiming that as the daughter of a white planter, she was owed freedom, she had been an indentured servant for longer than the stated course of her indenture, and she had been baptized into the Christian faith.[10]

Elizabeth lived in Virginia, where laws about slavery were still being codified, on the precipice of a country beginning to embrace race-based chattel slavery. She lived back when colonists were still trying to decide what the basis of slavery should be.

In her book *Christian Slavery*, Katharine Gerbner discusses an important shift: whereas, the division between the enslaved and the free was formerly Protestant/non-Protestant, it became white and Black. If the enslaved were in their condition because of their paganism, then sharing the gospel with them risked incurring their eventual freedom once they were baptized as brothers and sisters in Christ.

So, Elizabeth cited baptism as backing for her claim to freedom.

She also had her parentage in her corner. Prior to the 1660s, children inherited the condition of their fathers. If a white planter bore a child with an enslaved or indentured woman, that child would be free like his or her father. This followed British common law and held fathers responsible for providing for the needs of their children. If Elizabeth could prove white parentage, she could prove free parentage.

Finally, she was able to prove the length of her indenture had been ten years longer than it was supposed to be. Her servitude was never meant to be lifelong.

But less than ten years after Elizabeth won her freedom, laws began to change to make women like her more vulnerable than ever.

Legislation quickly closed the loopholes Elizabeth used to pursue her freedom. In 1662, a Virginia statute divorced from British common law, stating, "Negro women's children" would "serve according to the condition of the mother." In 1667, another statute declared that the baptism of slaves did not "exempt them from bondage."

Maryland, Virginia's neighbor, also set to work tightening the reins on the fledgling institution. In 1663, the state passed its first statute aimed at perpetuating lifelong slavery:

> Bee it Enacted by the Right Honorable the Lord Proprietary by the advice and Consent of the upper and lower house of this present General Assembly That all Negroes or other slaves already within the Province And **all Negroes and other slaves**

to bee hereafter imported into the Province shall serve Durante Vita [for life] And all Children born of any Negro or other slave shall be Slaves as their ffathers were for the terme of their lives.[11]

This legislation left Black women without protection from the sexual advances of the white planters who enslaved them. Any children resulting from such contact would not be seen as children of the planters but as property.

These acts are in no way a comprehensive list of legislation impacting Black women, but they offer a glimpse of the desperation many enslaved women faced. They lived in a patriarchal society where often the only patriarchs were white men. They were not offered the protection of legal marriage, or even custody of their own children. They could not testify against white (or Black) men in rape cases nor could they deny the sexual advances of masters or overseers. They could not protect their children, no matter who fathered them, or induce slaveholding fathers to provide for their progeny and secure their freedom.

In a society teeming with rules, regulations, and structures regarding what constituted godly womanhood, enslaved women were forced to live outside the bounds of Victorian rules. And free Black women were judged according to the abuse of their enslaved sisters.

This is the context in which Black abolitionist women sought to remind their listeners of their humanity. And it wasn't mere rhetoric; it was a true reminder of their worth in a country that prized a version of womanhood made unattainable to Black women—enslaved or free. The stereotypes that came to define Black enslaved women also impacted free Black women. And so, free Black abolitionist women applied their voices to impact perceptions of enslaved women as well.

Their speeches focused on encouraging the same virtue in Black women that white women promoted. From Maria Stewart, America's first Black woman political writer:

And such is the powerful force of prejudice. Let our girls possess **what amiable qualities of soul they may; let their characters be fair and spotless as innocence itself; let their natural taste and ingenuity be what they may;** it is impossible for scarce an individual of them to rise above the condition of servants. Ah! why is this cruel and unfeeling distinction? Is it merely because God has made our complexion to vary? If it be, O shame to soft, relenting humanity! "Tell it not in Gath! publish it not in the streets of Askelon!" Yet, after all, methinks were the American free people of color to turn their attention more assiduously to **moral worth and intellectual improvement, this would be the result: prejudice would gradually diminish, and the whites would be compelled to say, unloose those fetters!**[12]

Stewart was orphaned at a young age and grew up as an indentured servant to a Presbyterian minister. Though never enslaved, she knew the sting of being looked upon as less than. She made a place for herself in society, first in marriage to a respectable man, and then, after he died, through her abolitionist efforts. She believed Black respectability could finally compel white respect.

Sarah and Margaretta Forten could have shared how moral worth and intellectual improvement still left them reeling from the sting of racism. However, it was clear that Stewart sought the opportunity to show that Black women were just as capable of true womanhood as their white counterparts, if given the chance.

This is the tension Black women faced. Take a white counterpart: Frances Wright. Born in 1795, Wright spent her American career lambasting societal norms in ways Maria Stewart and the Forten sisters could have never dreamed. According to historian Holly Jackson, her name would become "shorthand for a festering fusion of interracial sex, Free Love, gender-bending, and atheism that threatened to bring down the Republic: 'that she-demon and unprincipled profligate, FANNY WRIGHT.'"[13]

Wright's brand of revolutionary feminism was not even a remote possibility for Maria, Sarah, Margaretta, and others.

Black women were already seen as unfeminine and therefore unworthy of respect. While Wright could cast off her femininity to make a statement, Stewart had to work overtime to even be considered feminine in the first place.

Make-or-Break Choices

Women like the Forten sisters warred on two fronts: as women wanting to take their place in a society that doubted their worth, and as Black women who were seen as inferior to white women's perceived virginal femininity.

Sarah and her other sister, Harriet, illustrated these battles through their marriages to the Purvis brothers. Of the two, Sarah seemed most likely to engage in abolitionist work for the rest of her days. She was the one who published her poems and treatises in *The Liberator*, after all. Where Harriet married at twenty-one, Sarah waited a bit longer, perhaps considering the singleness of their older sister, Margaretta.

Harriet's abolitionist work took flight after her marriage to Robert Purvis—a very vocal abolitionist and early feminist. With her husband, she became a conductor on the Underground Railroad and an important voice in the anti-slavery cause. The couple had eight children in their beautiful, English-style home in the Pennsylvania countryside, but Robert kept the home well-staffed with servants who helped to take the pressure off Harriet and freed her up for reform work.

With Robert's support, Harriet was active in both the anti-slavery and feminist struggles of the nineteenth century. She was a member of the National Woman Suffrage Association, as well as an organizer of the National Women's Rights Convention in Philadelphia in 1854, along with Margaretta, who never married.

At the 1869 National Women's Rights Convention, Robert showed how thoroughly he understood the delicate position of his Black wife by supporting women's suffrage.

Robert Purvis of Philadelphia said that he was willing to wait for the vote for himself and his sons and his race until women were also permitted to enjoy it. It was important to him that his daughter be enfranchised, since she bore the double curse of sex and race. He chided his son, Dr. Charles Purvis, for holding a narrow position, and reminded him that his sister Hattie also deserved to be enfranchised.[14]

Realizing that, as a Black woman, his daughter Hattie was working against two American prejudices, he sought the vote to protect her. This was the same sense he applied to his relationship with Harriet, who was able to pursue her passions in a way that many married women of the period would never have been able to imagine.

Conversely, Sarah married Robert Purvis's younger brother Joseph. She also had eight children but lived much more modestly than her sister, as a farmer's wife. Since Joseph wasn't as interested in abolition as his brother, Sarah's abolitionist work ceased. Her last abolitionist poem was written the year before her wedding, after which she faded from public view as the difficulties of married life and family overwhelmed her.

> Burdened with financial woes, and eight children, one of them, in the words of the Orphans' Court, "a Lunatic," she simply could not cope. Charlotte Forten visited her aunt in 1858 and reported: "As usual a scene of confusion and disorder greeted me." She could not help reflecting how differently everything was managed by Aunt Harriet at Byherry.[15]

Sarah would have died "homeless and destitute" after the death of her husband had it not been for the generosity of her mother and Margaretta. She died at the family home in 1884. Harriet had died many years before, comfortably at home.

Their older sister, Margaretta, died in 1875. Having never married, she was also able to continue in her activism unhampered by the needs of husband or children. She founded and ran a school, joined Harriet in suffragist work, and managed her father's estate after his death. Marriage to a man like Robert

MRS. FRANCIS E. W. HARPER.
See p. 753.

Purvis might have allowed her to continue such pursuits, but her younger sister Sarah's marriage proved the rarity of such a union.

Other activists, like Maria Stewart and Frances Ellen Watkins Harper, both pursued their abolitionist and suffragist passions outside the confines of a marriage. Stewart started her speaking career after becoming a young widow. Harper spoke and wrote before her marriage and then after her husband's death, giving up her public life to live quietly on a farm while her husband was alive.

Black women faced innumerable obstacles in freedom, the vast majority being needing to work, whether married or single, because of the discrepancy of pay between Black and white employees. In *Black Women Abolitionists*, Shirley Yee shares,

> Prevailing images of black women's sexuality and strength, combined with the fact that in freedom they provided vital economic support to families, led to stereotypes of the black family in the United States as matriarchal and, hence, pathological.[16]

Free Black women were subjected to the same exacting standards of true womanhood as their white counterparts while also grappling with the reality of systemic racism in America *and* the shocking imagery of enslaved Black womanhood in the South that led to further dehumanization in the North. A Black publication declared:

The moral or degraded condition of society depends solely upon the influence of woman, if she be virtuous, pious, industrious, her feet abiding in her own house, ruling her family well. . . . But if unhappily she should be the reverse, loud, clamorous, her feet wandering from the path of virtue, neglecting to rule her family, then indeed is the demoralizing effort of a bad influence felt in all avenues of her life.[17]

These restrictions had to be juggled alongside the work required of Black women both inside and outside the home. A formerly enslaved woman named Chloe Spear described this burden in a memoir:

After returning from a hard day's work, she many a time went to washing for her customers in the night, while her husband was taking his rest—extended lines across her room, and hung up her clothes to dry, while she retired to bed for a few hours; then arose, prepared breakfast and went out to work again, leaving her ironing to be done on her return at night. Cesar [her husband] having been accustomed to cooking, & could, on these occasions, wait upon himself and boarders, during her absence; but was quite willing that she should make ready a good super after she came home.[18]

Free Black women had to carry the burden of home and work—of American ideals of femininity inside the home and the reality of a hard day's work outside the home. They spoke out against slavery from a place of passion, but these speaking engagements were also how many of them were able to make a modest living.

When that young "lady of color" rose to the stage to declare that Black women *were* women and sisters, she did so in a context where being both Black and a woman rendered her status as someone created in the image of God debatable. Even the act of speaking out, of mounting a stage and using her voice for a just cause, flew in the face of her society's standards of femininity.

The Right Kind of Black Woman

On March 2, 1955, a fifteen-year-old girl named Claudette Colvin climbed onto a bus headed home from her high school, Booker T. Washington, in Montgomery, Alabama, aware of the mounting intensity of the civil rights movement. Just a few years earlier, her classmate Jeremiah Reeves had been convicted of the rape of Miss Mabel Ann Crowder.

Reeves had been only sixteen when police took him in for questioning, strapped him to an electric chair, and told him he would be electrocuted until he admitted to the rape. Colvin and other members of the community knew that Reeves and Crowder had been in a consensual relationship. But despite the involvement of Thurgood Marshall and the eventual overturning of the original conviction, Reeves was convicted again and executed for the rape.

By the time Claudette Colvin sat on that bus, she had written an entire paper about the problem of segregation in her community. When the bus filled up and the driver told her to give up her seat to a white passenger, she refused.

She later recalled:

> I could not move, because history had me glued to the seat. . . .
> It felt like Sojourner Truth's hands were pushing me down on one shoulder and Harriet Tubman's hands were pushing me down on another shoulder, and I could not move.[19]

Colvin's case galvanized civil rights organizers in Alabama. Following her arrest and conviction, they rallied around her until deciding she wasn't the kind of poster child they sought for their movement and stopped pursuing her case. At fifteen, she was considered too "feisty" and "uncontrollable"—and she lived on the wrong side of town.[20] When she became pregnant that summer, the powers that be felt even more confident in their decision to let Colvin's conviction stand.

The right kind of woman? Rosa Parks.

She was already an active participant in the civil rights movement, she was married, and she was respectable. When she refused to give up her seat that fateful December day, she did so in a calculated move to become the *right* kind of plaintiff. She became the face that history remembered for the movement.

The way they remembered her? As a demure, frail, middle-aged woman who was too tired to move.

They don't remember her as the fiery activist who helped organize The Committee for Equal Justice for Mrs. Recy Taylor, a young Black wife who was gang raped by white men in Abbeville, Alabama. They don't remember her risking her life to register to vote not one, not two, but *three* times. They don't remember her as the only woman working in the Montgomery chapter of the NAACP.

Just like they tend to forget Claudette Colvin ever existed.

"Am I not a woman and your sister?" is a multilayered question asked by Black women who are only allowed to fit into a certain mold in order to be deemed respectable. Claudette Colvin didn't fit that mold, but a reworked version of Rosa Parks certainly could.

In 1955, the image of the perfect housewife reigned supreme. She was polished, feminine, and demure. She wore pearls, heels, and coiffed hair while she ran her home.

And she was white.

That ideal of femininity did not extend to her Black maid, whether in the white lady's home or giving up her seat to the white lady on the bus.

"Am I not a woman and your sister?" was a question hundreds of Black women asked as they boycotted city buses, walking or carpooling to work for these white pictures of a version of femininity they were not often allowed.

They did the grunt work in a movement that would end segregation on Alabama's buses, in a movement helmed by Miss Rosa Parks and started by Miss Claudette Colvin.

They refused to give up their seats the same way Frances Ellen Watkins Harper refused to give up her place on a New England streetcar in 1858; the same way Ida B. Wells, who wrote about her experience, kept her spot on a streetcar in 1883.

> I have been insulted on several railroad cars. The other day, in attempting to ride in one of the city cars, after I had entered, the conductor came to me, and wanted me to go out on the platform. Now, was not that brave and noble? As a matter of course, I did not. Some one interfered, and asked or requested that I might be permitted to sit in a corner. I did not move, but kept the same seat. When I was about to leave, he refused my money, and I threw it down on the car floor, and got out, after I had ridden as far as I wished. Such impudence![21]

Black women had been demanding their seats for one hundred years before Claudette Colvin refused to move, and Claudette knew it. Ms. Maria Stewart, Ms. Frances Ellen Watkins Harper, and the Forten sisters all dotted Claudette's history. A movement of women boldly proclaiming their humanity on the buses of Alabama for the field hands in Mississippi from the lecterns of New England.

They declared they were made in the image of God before a world that refused to be convinced. And they demanded their seat at the table anyway.

4

"Marriage under Such a System"

For many, the concepts of marriage and family values bring to mind the "good old days" when men and women understood the importance of the home. Men left the house each day for work to provide and protect, whereas women stayed at home to guide and to keep. Children were shepherded in loving, two-parent environments that involved family worship around the dinner table and singing hymns by the fire.

This picture casts the past in a hazy, sepia-toned image of what "home" and "family" used to mean.

Often, when students think of this image of family, they conjure free white people who made enough money for wives to stay home, who lived far enough from the growing industrialism of American cities to have a homestead, and who knew how to read and write well enough to teach their own children.

Each descriptor shrinks the number of Americans who fit such a stereotypically idyllic home. And when you consider those enslaved in America, the number becomes minuscule.

Even stripped down to its barest descriptor—an intact family unit—this vision was untenable for most enslaved Black people in America, and the harsh truth of that reality is what will be discussed in this chapter.

The crawl space was a scant nine feet long and seven feet wide, with sloping ceilings not more than three feet high. The young woman could not turn to the right or left without brushing up against the walls of her narrow confines. Her only view of the world came through a peephole barely large enough to catch sight of a single star on a cloudless night. When it rained, the roof leaked. In the summer, it was oppressively hot, while the winter was painfully cold. Her youthful body showed signs of early aging as she marked her days in that tiny space: her back ached, her limbs spasmed, and she suffered a constant, bone-deep chill.

The woman occupied that tiny space for seven years. For more than two thousand days she lay there, constantly fearing capture, warring against discomfort, sharing that little attic with the mice who roamed around her. And in addition to the physical pain of her confinement, her heart was sick with the worry that hummed in the background of her every thought and deed: of detection, yes, but also for the children whom she watched through that little peephole.

She chose seven years of hiding in a dank crawl space to one more moment of enslavement. She chose to leave her children in the care of their white, slaveholding father rather than risk the wandering hands and leering eyes of her own master. She chose to lay down and hold her breath when the slave patrols wandered nearby, sometimes speaking *her* name, rather than spend another day enslaved.

When finally free, the woman penned her story under a pseudonym: Linda Brent. She told of her harrowing escape from that crawl space to freedom and her ultimate reunion with her children. She did her best to describe slavery as it was, walking that narrow tightrope of giving her readers enough detail to understand the peril of being a Black woman who was seen as a white man's property, while also endearing herself as a straitlaced and virtuous woman of Victorian standards.

"Linda," whose real name was Harriet Jacobs, took great care to cast the threat of violence—sexual and otherwise—in respectable terms, so much so that one of her editors remarked on it in a letter. Abolitionist Lydia Maria Child worried that the book, *Incidents in the Life of a Slave Girl*, wasn't salacious enough in its detailing of the grit of slavery.

> My object in writing at this time is to ask you to write what you can recollect of the outrages committed on the colored people, in Nat Turner's time. You say the reader would not believe what you saw "inflicted on men, women, and children, without the slightest ground of suspicion against them." What <u>were</u> those inflictions? Were any tortured to make them confess? and how? Where [sic] any killed? Please write down some of the most striking particulars, and let me have them to insert.[1]

Harriet Jacobs in 1894

Lydia Maria Child

Courtesy of the New York Public Library Digital Collections

Courtesy of Massachusetts Historical Society via Digital Commonwealth

81

Unsurprisingly, Jacobs and Child's relationship was sometimes fraught. Jacobs often felt that her editor's aid stepped over the line of proofreading, as was undoubtedly the case in this letter.

Nonetheless, as a newly free woman of color writing about her enslaved experiences, Jacobs balanced honesty about her encounters with living up to the incredibly high standards of decorum discussed in the previous chapter. She tried to share her story while also shielding some of her dignity.

This balancing act was incredibly difficult for Harriet Jacobs in freedom.

It was nigh unto impossible for her sisters still in slavery.

Amalgamation Literature

The enslavers of the South were adamant that their property should not have access to abolitionist literature. Never mind the fact that most of the enslaved could not read, thanks to a law designed to keep them from reading such literature or even finding too many freedom stories in the Bible. The mere *possession* of reading materials, regardless of whether they were being read, was dangerous enough.

Shortly before Harriet Jacobs ran to freedom, Mississippi passed a law with the intent of keeping enslaved women like her from getting too many notions of freedom:

> In 1830 Mississippi passed a law making it illegal for whites and blacks to "print, write, circulate, or put forth . . . any book, paper, magazine, pamphlet, handbill or circular" that contained "any sentiment, doctrine, advice or inuendoes calculated to produce a disorderly, dangerous or rebellious disaffection among the colored population of this state, or in anywise to endanger the peace of society, by exciting riots and rebellion among said population." Whites who were found guilty of this offense would receive a fine of up to $1,000 and a minimum three-month prison

term, with a twelve-month maximum. Blacks, however, whether free or enslaved, who were found guilty "shall suffer death."[2]

White slaveholders of the South saw abolitionist literature as such a profound danger that they would kill their own enslaved property—worth hundreds and sometimes thousands of dollars—if they were caught sharing such literature.

Slaveholders knew well the danger that lay in the ideals of liberty, and they were hell-bent on keeping such literature out of the hands of the enslaved.

In 1839, Francis Philpot published a proslavery pamphlet with the title *Facts for White Americans, with a Plain Hint for Dupes, and a Bone to Pick for White Nigger Demagogues and Amalgamation Abolitionists, including the Parentage, Brief Career, and Execution, of Amalgamation Abolitionism.* His was one of many texts aimed at alerting slaveholders to their worst nightmares of emancipation: amalgamation.

Noah Webster's 1828 dictionary defines *amalgamation* as "the mixing or blending of different things."[3] Put plainly, the amalgamation white planters feared was the intermingling of Black and white people in the South.

In *Closer to Freedom*, Stephanie M. H. Camp describes an 1839 print meant to similarly raise Southerners' blood pressure at what abolitionists *really* wanted:

An earlier 1839 print, Practical Amalgamation, depicts a lovely and dainty white woman who sits on the lap of a guitar-playing black man and kisses his elongated face on the unseemly, large lips. By their side, a round-shouldered, bare-headed white man bends his lanky legs to kneel and kiss the hand of a rotund and overheated black woman. The whites here do more than mix with blacks; they give themselves up to them, revealing themselves (the white man especially) to be weak and contemptible. Even the black and white dogs on the left side of the print seem to know better: they sit beside each other, but the black dog appears to growl at the white dog, who responds with dignified aloofness. These images reveal the worst that abolition meant to slaveholders—amalgamation of the black and white races.[4]

The irony of this rabid fear, of course, was that the "amalgamation of the black and white races" had been happening on plantations throughout the South for centuries. Harriet Jacobs ran for freedom for many reasons, the principal of which were the unwanted sexual advances of her enslaver. Her children had been fathered by another white slaveholder who Jacobs took up with in hopes of rebuffing her own enslaver's advances. Recalling this tactical decision, she bemoaned:

But, O, ye happy women, whose purity has been sheltered from childhood, who have been free to choose the objects of your affection, whose homes are protected by law, do not judge the poor desolate slave girl too severely! If slavery had been abolished, I, also, could have married the man of my choice; I could

PRACTICAL AMALGAMATION.

have had a home shielded by the laws; and I should have been spared the painful task of confessing what I am now about to relate; but all my prospects had been blighted by slavery. I wanted to keep myself pure; and, under the most adverse circumstances, I tried hard to preserve my self-respect; but I was struggling alone in the powerful grasp of the demon Slavery; and the monster proved too strong for me. I felt as if I was forsaken by God and man; as if all my efforts must be frustrated; and I became reckless in my despair.[5]

Jacobs's desperation flies in the face of contemporary representations of Black female sexuality. Even anti-slavery activists fell into the trap of thinking of Black women as more sexually permissive than their white counterparts. Abolitionist James Redpath stated:

Again, I am a white man, and I know that mulatto women almost always refuse to cohabit with the blacks; are often averse to a sexual connection with persons of their own *shade*; but are gratified by the criminal advances of Saxons, whose intimacy, they hope, may make them the mothers of children almost white—which is the quadroon girl's ambition: is it likely, then, that a young man will resist temptation, when it comes in the form of a beautiful slave maiden, who has perhaps—as is often the case—a fairer complexion than his own, and an exquisitely handsome figure?

It is neither likely, nor *so*! It is a crime against morality to be silent on such subjects. Slavery, *not* Popery, is the foul Mother of Harlots![6]

Jacobs's story contradicts Redpath's characterization of "mulatto women," who were the offspring of enslavers and the enslaved. She was not "gratified" by her enslaver Norcum's "criminal advances" but disgusted by them. Amalgamation was not her goal—freedom was.

But that amalgamation was an inescapable part of being both enslaved and a woman.[7]

The Legal Foundation of Slavery

In her book *Bound in Wedlock*, Tera W. Hunter writes:

> The legal foundation for racial slavery in Anglo-America was constituted in the subjugation of black women. African-American women's sexuality was a central axis of power of masters over slaves, the means by which gender, racial, and material oppression were enmeshed. The diminution of motherhood, the negation of fatherhood, the disavowal of sexual violence, and the invalidation of marriage became an interlocking system of white dominance over blacks that would be further codified in the laws and carried out in everyday practice for centuries.[8]

When the Virginia law passed declaring slavery matrilineal, the plight of Black enslaved women solidified in a terrifying way. They were viewed as sexual objects, yes, but also as a boon to white slaveholders. Their fertility became the basis of the American slave trade, especially after the transatlantic trade was discontinued in 1808.

When docking in America's harbors became illegal for slave ships (at least officially[9]), one might have expected a dip in the supply of human chattel in the country. In fact, the number of enslaved Black Americans grew by leaps and bounds from 1808 to 1860, even more so than it had during the years when chattel was being brought directly from Africa.

Black women bore property for their enslavers. In an 1820 letter to John Wayles Eppes, Thomas Jefferson remarked:

> I consider a woman who brings a child every two years as more profitable than the best man of the farm. What she produces is an addition to the capital, while his labors disappear in mere consumption.[10]

Black women held immeasurable value as mothers, but as previously discussed, their motherhood was not valued in the same way as their white counterparts. Instead, Black women were seen as inherently *un*-nurturing, even when conscribed to nursing the white children of their masters.

Because of the squalid living conditions in the slave quarters, Black children were exposed to "malaria, influenza, whooping cough, lockjaw, and winter fevers,"[11] which created an incredibly high mortality rate for enslaved infants and children. Still, when Black children died, it was attributed to negligence by their mothers.

Enslaved women also lived with the constant knowledge that, at any moment, they could be separated from their children.

> Historians estimate the long-distance domestic trade broke up one in three enslaved marriages and separated one fifth of children from their parents. Because women were frequently sold as "fetishized commodities" to be the sexual slaves of men, their exploitation within the domestic slave trade was both gendered and multifaceted. Enslaved women were exploited and sold as laborers, reproducers, and forced concubines known as "fancy girls."[12]

Motherhood presented a barrier to self-emancipation. Enslaved mothers who weren't separated from their children forcibly by sale were far less likely to abandon their children than their male counterparts. When enslaved women tried to escape with their children, their risk of recapture increased exponentially.

Enslaved motherhood was fraught with terror in a time when white motherhood was lauded as an almost saintly endeavor. Christian motherhood was treated as the crown of white family life while Black families were being systematically torn apart by the slave trade. And the enslaved felt this dissonance deeply, particularly when trying to form familial ties of their own.

The Slave Family

Henry Bibb married his wife, Malinda, in 1838. The son of an enslaved woman and a senator, Bibb was able to receive some education as a child, a rarity among his fellow enslaved Kentuckians, before the school he attended was shut down to quell enslaved literacy. Henry and Malinda were able to marry for love unlike so many other enslaved couples, brought together for their enslavers to breed the strongest stock possible.

Of his marriage to Malinda, Henry said:

> There is no legal marriage among the slaves of the South; I never saw nor heard of such a thing in my life, and I have been through seven of the slave states. A slave marrying according to law, is a thing unknown in the history of American Slavery. And be it known to the disgrace of our country that every slaveholder, who is the keeper of a number of slaves of both sexes, is also the keeper of a house or houses of ill-fame. Licentious white men, can and do, enter at night or day the lodging places of slaves; break up the bonds of affection in families; destroy all their domestic and social union for life; and the laws of the country afford them no protection.[13]

"Licentious white men" eventually came between Henry and his bride. He was allowed to marry Malinda under one condition, which he considered too vulgar to write down in his memoir.[14] "If my wife," he wrote, "must be exposed to the insults and licentious passions of wicked slavedrivers and overseers; if she must bear the stripes of the lash laid on by an unmerciful tyrant; if this is to be done with impunity, which is frequently done by slaveholders and their abettors, Heaven forbid that I should be compelled to witness the sight."[15]

Henry left Malinda and his young daughter, Mary Frances, in 1837 with the goal of escaping and raising enough money to purchase their freedom. However, his efforts stopped abruptly in the winter of 1845 when he learned that Malinda and Mary Frances had been sold to Louisiana, and that Malinda was living in "a state of adultery" with her master there.

> From that time I gave her into the hands of an all-wise Providence. As she was then living with another man, I could no longer regard her as my wife. After all the sacrifices, sufferings, and risks which I had run, striving to rescue her from the grasp of slavery; every prospect and hope was cut off. She has ever since been regarded as theoretically and practically dead to me as a wife, for she was living in a state of adultery, according to the law of God and man. [16]

Bibb seemed to understand that Malinda's status might not be one of her own choosing, stating that he brought "no charge of it against her, for I know not all the circumstances connected with the case."[17] But because Malinda wrote to her family that she was happy, well-treated by her new master, and that she had given up on Henry, he gave up on her. "In view of all the facts and circumstances connected with this matter, I deem further comments and explanations unnecessary on my part."[18]

Henry remarried a free woman in 1848. His words about that union reveal the wound left by his marriage with Malinda:

> Not in slave-holding style, which is a mere farce, without the sanction of law or gospel; but in accordance with the laws of God and our country. My beloved wife is a bosom friend, a helpmeet, a loving companion in all the social, moral, and religious relations of life. She is to me what a poor slave's wife can never be to her husband while in the condition of a slave; for she can not be true to her husband contrary to the will of her master. She can neither be pure nor virtuous, contrary to the will of her master. She dare not refuse to be reduced to a state of adultery at the will of her master; from the fact that the slaveholding law, customs and teachings are all against the poor slaves.[19]

89

Bibb's feelings were clearly complex. He understood that most enslaved women dared not refuse the advances of their masters or overseers, but Malinda's resignation struck such a chord in him that he considered their union effectively divorced, so much so that he stopped trying to purchase her freedom or that of his own daughter.

Bibb was one of countless enslaved and formerly enslaved men who found themselves unable to protect the women they loved from the system that owned them. In his book *Rethinking Rufus*, Thomas A. Foster outlines the difficulty of enslaved men to feel they could properly care for and protect their wives, whether from the exceedingly violent punishment enslaved women often incurred or the sexual advances of their enslavers. He quotes a formerly enslaved man, Henry Brown:

> Talk of marriage under such a system. Why, the owner of a Turkish harem, or the keeper of a house of ill-fame, might as well allow the inmates of their establishments to marry as for a Southern slaveholder to do the same. Marriage, as is well known, is the voluntary and perfect union of one man with one woman, without depending upon the will of a third party. This never can take place under slavery, for the moment a slave is allowed to form such a connection as he chooses, the spell of slavery is dissolved.[20]

Hunter builds upon this idea in *Bound in Wedlock*:

> As chattel, slaves were objects, not subjects. Marriage for them was not an inviolable union between two people but an institution defined and controlled by the superior relationship of master to slave. The interventions of what I call the "third flesh" did not make for a legitimate union that could be easily reconciled in the growing body of law or in Christian traditions derivative of Western Europe.[21]

Scholar Zakiyyah Jackson puts it a different way: "Western science and philosophy viewed Black people as empty vessels, as non-beings, and as ontological zeros."[22] Though some theologians might have given a tacit nod to the fact that the enslaved were also human and, therefore, created in God's image, the lived reality treated them as little more than cattle. Their family unions were only valuable insofar as they were lucrative.

Family and the *Imago Dei*

In 1606, Puritan theologian William Perkins wrote:

> The ende of marriage is fourefold. The first is, procreation of children, for the propagation and continuance of man upon the earth, Gen. 1.28. . . . The second is the procreation of an holy seed, whereby the Church of God may be kept holy and chaste, and there may alwaies be a holy companie of men, that may worship and serve God in the Church from age to age, Malach. 2.15. . . . The third is, that after the fall of mankind, it might be a soveraigne means to subdue and slake the burning lusts of the flesh, I Cor. 7.2. . . . The fourth ende is, that the parties married may thereby perform the duties of their callings, in better and more comfortable manner, Prov. 31.1.[23]

These ideals of marriage prevailed throughout the seventeenth, eighteenth, and nineteenth centuries. Marriage existed (1) for procreation, (2) for the training up of a godly seed, (3) for a holy sexual outlet, and (4) for the couple to join together and live out their callings. In nineteenth-century America, a wife's calling was most likely confined to that of a sympathetic and encouraging partner to her husband in whatever he endeavored, along with raising her children.

These ideas of matrimony and family life coexisted with the rise of chattel slavery, both in Puritan England as well as America. While the roles of white husbands and wives were becoming culturally entrenched in the United States, so was the worth of Black, enslaved marriages.

The Biblical Blueprint and the Reality

In Genesis 1, God creates Adam and Eve and declares that the two human beings have been made "in our image" (v. 26). They are two complementary halves of a whole: Adam cannot fulfill the mission given to him by God without Eve, who was created *from* Adam. In this way, God elevates the institution of marriage, making it a special, even mysterious way for human beings to understand a glimpse of how his Son, Jesus, loves his bride, the church.

This mystery was the basis of many an American sermon, all while Americans of the South undermined the marital relationships of the enslaved. Marriage was sacred . . . until it involved a Black man or woman. Parenthood was a high and holy calling . . . until the children of the enslaved could fetch a good price at market.

This dual perception of family for the enslaved and their enslavers did not go unnoticed, even as it was largely ignored in the South.

Thomas Paine, political activist and author of *Common Sense*, wrote a pamphlet decrying slavery at the height of America's founding. He equated slavery to murder, and lambasted "Christianized people" who approved of a practice contrary to "the light of nature, to every principle of Justice and humanity." And he gave special attention to talking about how slavery specifically impacted families:

> So monstrous is the making and keeping them slaves at all, abstracted from the barbarous usage they suffer, and the many evils attending the practice; as selling husbands away from wives, children from parents, and from each other, in violation of sacred and natural ties; and opening the way for adulteries, incests, and many shocking consequences, for all of which the guilty Masters must answer to the final Judge.[24]

The separation of families was so endemic to slavery that it became a mainstay of abolitionist outcry against the practice. How could people who claimed to fear God and revere marriage and family simultaneously undermine the families of people they owned?

The answer is, of course, buried in the question. This ownership—"monstrous," as Paine called it—was itself an affront to the humanity of those owned. Affirming in speech that the enslaved were made in the image of God while treating enslaved families in ways that undermined God's law and nature betrays a fundamental misunderstanding of the *imago Dei*.

How could slaveholders believe their chattel was made in God's image while profaning that image through the lived realities of chattel slavery?

Both things could not be true at the same time.

Rape and Resistance

In her book *At the Dark End of the Street: Black Women, Rape, and Resistance*, Danielle L. McGuire discusses the terrorism employed through the sexual violation of both Black men and women.

> When African Americans tested their freedom during Reconstruction, former slaveholders and their sympathizers used rape as a "weapon of terror" to dominate the bodies and minds of African-American men and women. Interracial rape was not only used to uphold the white patriarchal power but was also deployed as a justification for lynching black men who challenged the Southern status quo. In addition to the immediate physical danger African Americans faced, sexual and racial violence functioned as a tool of coercion, control, and harassment.[25]

During slavery, rape against Black women was not considered a crime, whether carried out by white or Black men. Even after slavery, rape of Black women was seldom punished in the Jim Crow South. While activism around lynching ramped up throughout the early twentieth century, women like Fannie Barrier Williams, Ida B. Wells, and Anna Julia Cooper testified about the sexual abuse and harassment faced by so many Black women in the South.

"The rape of helpless Negro girls, which began in slavery days, still continues without reproof from church, state, or press," Ida B. Wells said.

Fannie Barrier Williams talked of the "shameful fact that I am constantly in receipt of letters from the still unprotected women of the south."

Anna Julia Cooper declared that Black women engaged in a "painful, patient, and silent toil. . . . To gain title to the bodies of their daughters."[26]

Harriet Jacobs wrote of her own sexual abuse in the forthright, yet ladylike voice of a Victorian woman. But the abuse routinely perpetuated against Black women throughout the eighteenth, nineteenth, and twentieth centuries in America was anything but.

On the night of May 2, 1959, Florida A&M University student Betty Jean Owens was kidnapped by four white men. They held her friends at gunpoint, took her to the woods, and raped her seven times. When the case went to trial, the world was watching. Recy Taylor's 1944 trial had garnered enough media attention to result in the conviction of her rapists, but they served minimal time and paid small fines. Over fifteen hundred students gathered to show their support of Betty Jean and to demand justice.

The day of the trial, four hundred spectators gathered to watch Betty Jean stand up to her rapists.

Restless spectators, squeezed into every corner of the segregated courthouse, crowded back into their seats when jurors emerged after three hours of deliberation with a decision. An additional three hundred African Americans held a silent vigil outside. A. H. King, the jury foreman and a local plantation owner, slowly read aloud the jury's decision for all four defendants: "guilty with a recommendation for mercy." The recommendation for mercy saved the four men from the electric chair and, according to the *Baltimore Afro-American*, "made it inescapably clear that the death penalty for rape is only for colored men accused by white women."[27]

When Betty Jean's attackers were sentenced to life in prison, it was the first time a white man was ever given such a harsh penalty for the rape of a Black woman. In a nation that perpetuated slavery through kidnapping and rape for over one hundred and eighty years, this moment was a significant one.

In a nation where fourteen-year-old Emmett Till had been brutally murdered for allegedly whistling at a white woman only four years earlier, the conviction signaled progress. Till's murderers were still roaming free when Betty Jean's kidnappers were imprisoned.

But something about the victory rang hollow. When Betty Jean was asked about the sentencing, she said, "It is something. I am grateful that twelve white men believed the truth, but I still wonder what they would have done if one of our boys raped a white girl."[28]

But Betty Jean did not have to wonder.

No one had to wonder. Seventy percent of the men who received the death penalty in the South from 1910 to 1950 were Black along with 90 percent of the men executed for rape in the United States between 1930 and 1967.[29] In 1927, Governor George Hays of Arkansas said the death penalty was needed to address "the negro problem." Between 1877 and 1950, more than 4,440 terror lynchings were carried out in America.

Betty Jean's attackers were punished, but not at the level she believed they would have been punished had they been Black men. And it left her wondering aloud if the disparity was a matter of perceived worth.

When abolitionists rallied for the rights of Black families, their rallying cries encompassed so much: the right to bodily autonomy, the right to their own sexuality, the right to raise their own children, the right to protect their spouses, the right to work and earn an honest wage, the right to set up a family structure without third-party involvement.

This is why they brought up the separation of families, because they saw family as one of the basic results of the *imago Dei*. It is why they focused on "virtue" (sexuality), because they witnessed the extreme hypocrisy of a nation obsessed with female purity unless the women were Black.

This is why Black love and marriage, Black fidelity and parenthood, were in and of themselves a radical proclamation of *imago Dei* against overwhelming odds. These institutions were, and are, worth protecting.

5

"Not a Single Presbyterian Negro"

Black abolitionist pastors blazed a trail of revolutionary activism, despite the roadblocks many of them faced when it came to being recognized by their denominations. Each of these stories centers on the pastor of a thriving body of believers who simultaneously preached the Word in the pulpit on Sunday and advocated for the enslaved throughout their lives. The enslaved faced even greater roadblocks in their quest for religious freedom south of the Mason-Dixon Line.

It's Sunday morning in 1839.

In New York, Theodore Sedgewick Wright steps into the lectern at the First Colored Presbyterian Church. He has ministered there since 1830 and is known for his theologically robust sermons. The first year he pastored the church, its membership doubled, and the growth would continue throughout his lifelong tenure. Born to free Black parents in 1797, Wright is a graduate of Princeton Theological Seminary, an outspoken advocate for abolition, and a theologically astute Presbyterian through and through. Wright preaches the entire Word of God faithfully and without reservation, which means when he talks about oppression, he condemns the institution of slavery with wholehearted loathing. He's in good company. That same Sunday, Thomas Gardner at a Presbyterian church in Philadelphia, Daniel Payne at a Lutheran church in New York, and Black ministers in the relatively new African Methodist Episcopal denomination in Baltimore all preach the Word of God to their Black parishioners.

On that same day, in the small town of Louisville, Mississippi, an enslaved man named Adam sits under the preaching of a white pastor. He and fellow enslaved members of First Baptist sit in a separate section from the white members. Though allowed to attend the church alongside white Mississippians, it is clear to Adam, as well as the rest of the enslaved church members, that outside the church's walls, their brotherhood in Christ does not afford them rights or privileges in the cotton fields. Likely, Adam's enslaver hopes that slavery will be a "useful opiate"[1] to keep him in line. In fact, that Bible was often used at this church and elsewhere to encourage slaves to obey their masters.

Later that evening, in rural Louisiana, an enslaved woman waits for the last light to go out in the Big House. When it does, she tiptoes out of her cabin, steps light, breath hitched, and picks her way along a path toward the woods. Moving deeper and deeper into the cover of the trees, she follows the muffled sounds of a drum and a harmonica, low voices, soul-deep wails, and shuffling feet. When she finally makes it to the clearing, she finds other slaves gathered in the middle of a ring shout, a cluster of worshipers gathered in a circle, singing, dancing, and chanting together in worship. If they are caught, they will be flogged. The enslaved are not allowed to meet without a

98

white person present. But meet they do, as often as they can, to listen to the slave preacher recite long pieces of biblical text from memory, and to praise the God they trust will one day bring them freedom.

Protestant Supremacy

In her book *Christian Slavery*, Katharine Gerbner makes a compelling case for how "Protestant supremacy" fed what later became "white supremacy" regarding how most of the free citizenry view the enslaved in America:

> Protestant Supremacy was the predecessor of White Supremacy, an ideology that emerged after the codification of racial slavery. . . . They constructed a caste system based on Christian status, in which "heathenish" slaves were afforded no rights or privileges while Catholics, Jews, and non-conforming Protestants were viewed with suspicion and distrust, but granted more protections.[2]

When white colonists first began to import enslaved Africans, they often based their enslavement on the fact that the Africans were "heathens." In this way, Protestant slaveholders could cast themselves as the Israelites of old, conquering people groups abroad (and Indigenous nations locally) as their gospel birthright. Protestant settlers, according to Gerbner, based their dominance over the enslaved class on their religious superiority.

> White supremacist racial thought emerged in the fifteenth century and dramatically shaped the interactions between Europeans and Africans. Religious divisions drawn by Europeans, between followers of Christ and heathens, helped define the meaning of race. "European" or "English" meant "Christian" and "white." "African," by contrast, meant "heathen," despite the fact that many Africans had been Christianized, and large

portions of North and sub-Saharan Africa had fallen under the sway of Islam.[3]

But when Elizabeth Key sued for freedom based on her baptism, she revealed a gaping hole in this plan. What would happen to the slave class if they became Christians? Was it lawful to keep brothers and sisters in Christ in bondage? And how could slaveholders be sure that professions of faith among the enslaved were sincere and not just a ploy to achieve their freedom?

In response to these questions, many slaveholders neglected the religious education of the enslaved—at least, those who did not come to American shores as Christians.

Notably, many West African nations had already been exposed to the gospel when the slave trade began. Initially, when Christianity began to spread like wildfire in the first century, it encountered Africa before it ever touched the West. Though West African nations might not have seen mass conversion during Christianity's initial spread, countries like the Kingdom of Kongo (present-day Angola) were converted to Catholicism as early as the fifteenth century. However, as Catholics, their religious expression was still often considered beneath that of their Protestant enslavers.

American slaveholders reasoned that if they kept Christianity away from their chattel, they would eliminate the insecurity that came with Christianized property. As historian Paul Harvey states:

> In theory, non-Christians could be enslaved; Christians could not. The earliest process of racializing diverse peoples involved ignoring, denying, or denigrating their religions. This held true both for Christian and Islamic enslavers.[4]

A Maryland act of 1671 scolded planters for not sharing the gospel with their slaves for fear of baptism leading to their freedom. The legislation claimed that this fear was based on an "ungrounded apprehension" that by "becoming Christians they and the issue of their bodies [their children] are actually manumitted and made free." Slaveholders were assured that

> where any Negro or Negroes Slave or Slaves being in Servitude or bondage is are or shall become Christian or Christians and . . . Receive the Holy Sacrament of Babtizme before or after his her or their Importation into this Province the same is not nor shall or ought the same be . . . taken to be or amount unto a manumission or freeing Inlarging or discharging any such . . . Negroes Slave or Slaves . . . or their Issue . . . from . . . their Servitude . . . any opinion or other matter or thing to the Contrary in any wise Notwithstanding.[5]

Maryland was the first state to speak up about how baptism did not confer freedom, but it was far from the last. Slowly, perceptions of slavery in America began to shift. It was not *religious* but *racial* inferiority that consigned Africans to bondage.

Still, many planters were hesitant to share the gospel with the enslaved.

> The shift from "Christian" to "white" was halting and incomplete. Even as Protestant slave owners redefined mastery in racial terms, they continued to exclude the majority of enslaved men and women from Christian rites. The sustained resistance to slave conversion demonstrates the persistent connection between Protestantism and whiteness. The fledgling ideology of White Supremacy emerged from the foundation of Protestant Supremacy and it would take decades before slave owners felt secure enough in their whiteness to accept widespread slave conversion.[6]

By 1730, few of the enslaved were granted access to churches, and those who were, remained in legislated illiteracy, unable to read the Bible for themselves.[7]

101

But something was brewing. The Great Awakening was spreading across America, and its concentration on bringing as many souls to faith as possible blurred class, gender, and racial lines. The enslaved were converted to the Christian religion in greater numbers than ever before.

In the South, slave religion was still treated with distrust. While baptism was no longer a surefire prerequisite on the road to freedom, the meeting of the enslaved was viewed with suspicion. In the one hundred years between the Great Awakening and Nat Turner's rebellion, at least three slave rebellions were launched by enslaved men who were also preachers and used the Bible as the impetus for their revolts.

An underground church developed during this time, an "invisible institution," as Albert J. Raboteau describes it in his book *Slave Religion*. The enslaved cobbled together a robust Christian ethic despite the cupidity of their enslavers.

> Separate and apart from the official churches, slaves conducted secret religious ceremonies in the slave quarters and in "brush harbors," the name given to small gathering spots in the backwoods protected by canopies of tree branches. In these secluded places, which slaves sometimes referred to as "hush harbors" because of their secrecy, black ministers preached in a manner they could not display in front of whites.[8]

Christianity became a mainstay for Black Americans—both enslaved and free. And it informed them of the rights and privileges of people made in the image of God wherever it landed.

Slavery Brutalizes Man

Daniel Payne did not set out to be a minister—at least, not at first.

Born of free parents in Charleston, South Carolina, Payne started as a teacher. He was passionate about educating his

Black students. His school quickly gained a reputation as especially rigorous, and some in South Carolina balked at his teaching Black children subjects like Greek and Latin. Nevertheless, Payne persisted in educating young minds until a South Carolina law passed in 1834, outlawing the education of both enslaved *and* free Black children. Payne fled the South, and after pursuing a seminary education to become a Lutheran minister, was ordained in 1839.

The day of his ordination, he preached a sermon titled "Slavery Brutalizes Man" in support of a synodical report to end slavery in America. He rooted his objections to slavery in his Christian faith, stating:

This being God created but a little lower than the angels, and crowned him with glory and honor; but slavery hurls him down from his elevated position, to the level of brutes, strikes this crown of glory from his head and fastens upon his neck the galling yoke, and compels him to labor like an ox, through summer's sun and winter's snow, without remuneration.[9]

Educated at the Lutheran Theological Seminary in Pennsylvania, Payne had the theological mettle to attack slavery as the anti-Christian institution that it was. In his sermon, he uses verse 7 from this passage in Hebrews:

For it was not to angels that God subjected the world to come, of which we are speaking. It has been testified somewhere,

"What is man, that you are mindful of him,
   or the son of man, that you care for him?
You made him for a little while lower than the angels;
   you have crowned him with glory and honor,
putting everything in subjection under his feet."

Now in putting everything in subjection to him, he left nothing outside his control. At present, we do not yet see everything in subjection to him. But we see him who for a little while was made lower than the angels, namely Jesus, crowned with glory and honor because of the suffering of death, so that by the grace of God he might taste death for everyone. (vv. 5–9 ESV)

Payne goes on to outline how Southern notions of Black inferiority bar Black fathers from teaching their children about Jesus and, further, bar preachers from illuminating the entire counsel of God's Word in the South:

> I knew a pious slave in Charleston who was a licensed exhorter in the Methodist Episcopal Church; this good man was in the habit of spending his Saturday nights on the surrounding plantations, preaching to the slaves. One night, as usual, he got into a canoe, sailed upon James' Island. While in the very act of preaching the unsearchable riches of Christ to dying men, the patrols seized him and whipped him in the most cruel manner, and compelled him to promise that he would never return to preach again to those slaves.[10]

In contrast to Payne, Robert Louis Dabney, an 1846 graduate of Union Seminary and a respected Presbyterian minister, argued that slavery was actually of religious benefit to the enslaved.

> A reference to the statistics of the religious denominations of the country shows that slavery has made about a half a million, one in every six of these pagan savages, a professor of Christianity. The whole number of converted pagans, now church members, connected with the mission churches of the Protestant world, is supposed to be about 191,000, a goodly and encouraging number indeed. But compare these converted pagans with the 500,000 converts from the pagan Africans among us, and we see that through the civilizing agency of domestic slavery, the much-slandered Christianity of the South has done far more for the salvation of heathen men than all the religious

enterprise of Protestant Christendom! And this is, no doubt, but the dawn of the brighter day, which the benevolent affection of the masters will light up around the black population, if they are not interfered with by the schemes of a frantic fanaticism.[11]

Dabney, who would go on to be a Confederate army chaplain and biographer of Stonewall Jackson, states that in addition to half a million converts from "pagan" Africa, slavery has been a "civilizing agency."

Yet Dabney's a observations about the Christianizing influence of slavery do not jibe with Daniel Payne's characterization of slavery. Nor do they match up with Nat Turner's experience of slavery, James Forten's experience of freedom, or the barbarism experienced by many enslaved women at the hands of their enslavers.

From the New York Public Library

BISHOP DANIEL A. PAYNE.

Indeed, on that last point, Payne has much to say:

> In a word, it is in view of man's moral agency that God commands him to shun vice, and practice virtue. But what female slave can do this? I lived twenty-four years in the midst of slavery and never knew but six female slaves who were reputedly virtuous! What profit is to the female slave that she is disposed to be virtuous? Her will, like her body, is not her own; they are both at the pleasure of her master; and he brands them at his will. So it subverts the moral government of God.[12]

If the slavery of the South instilled Christian virtues in the enslaved, why would female slaves find it hard to remain "virtuous"? Why would it be so difficult for them to retain autonomy of their bodies? Why would the pleasure of a master be an issue for an enslaved woman if those pleasures are restrained by the missional hand of a benevolent enslaver?

The hypocrisy of enslavers was no secret among their contemporaries. Yet modern imaginations have sometimes concocted an idyllic vision of slaveholders discipling the enslaved. In reality, they often held their perceived piety in one hand and a whip in the other.

Not a Single Presbyterian Negro

In 1867, shortly after emancipation, a resolution was put forth at General Assembly:[13]

> Whereas the paper upon the subject of the coloured people, adopted by the last General Assembly, has been erroneously construed by some as teaching the doctrine that coloured men, possessing the qualifications required by the standards of our Church and the word of God, should not be ordained to the full work of the Gospel ministry, simply because they belong to the negro race; therefore,
>
> *Resolved*, That the General Assembly be overtured to declare that the Church is Christ's universal kingdom; that its doors are open alike to all those who love the Lord Jesus, and that ordination to the work of the Gospel ministry is to be given to all those called of God to, and qualified for the work, without respect of persons.[14]

Some Presbyterians believed it was time to end the injustice of withholding ordination from ministers based on their race. They wanted to correct what had plagued many Southern presbyteries since their inception and extend the hand of fellowship and the opportunity for the pastorate to both white and Black believers.

Dabney presented an opinion denouncing this overture for many reasons, one of which is especially interesting, considering the Sunday scenes of 1839:

While I greatly doubt whether a single Presbyterian negro will ever be found to come fully up to that high standard of learning, manners, sanctity, prudence, and moral weight and acceptability, which our constitution requires, and which this overture *professes* to honour so impartially; I clearly foresee that, no sooner will it be passed than it will be made the pretext for a partial and odious lowering of our standard, in favour of negroes.

He denounced Black men's abilities while those abilities had been on display for decades in pulpits all over America. Dabney went on to say:

I oppose the entrusting of the destinies of our Church, in any degree whatever, to black rulers, because that race is not trustworthy for such position. There may be *a few exceptions*; (I do not believe I have ever seen one, though I have known negroes whom I both respected and loved, in their proper position) but I ask emphatically: Do legislatures frame general laws to meet the rare exceptions? or do they adjust them to the general average? Now, who that knows the negro, does not know that his is a subservient race; that he is made to follow, and not to lead; and his temperament, idiosyncrasy, and social relation, make him untrustworthy as a depositary of power?

Dabney argued that such a Negro *might* exist, but he's never seen one, and that leadership was against the very nature of Negroes—"his temperament, idiosyncrasy, and social relation, make him untrustworthy as a depositary of power."

Dabney made these statements in 1867. But Thomas Sedgewick Wright graduated from Princeton Theological Seminary in 1828. He was the first Black man to attend any seminary in the United States and far from the last. Other notable Black Presbyterian ministers who served before this speech include Samuel Eli Cornish, Charles Ray, Henry Highland Garnet, Amos

Beman, James W. C. Pennington, John Chavis, John Gloucester, and Charles W. Gardner. Most of them served thriving Black churches in New England long before the onset of the Civil War that helped launch Dabney into fame.

Whether or not Dabney was aware of these men, he saw slavery as their natural state and Christian education as one of the "bonuses" of American chattel slavery. Yet when that education led to the likes of Pennington, Gloucester, and Garnet, Dabney felt their supporters had become so "interested about this unfortunate race" that they had taken "leave of their own good sense" and grown "extravagant, hasty, and inconsiderate" in their attempts to ordain Black preachers.[15]

Contrast Dabney's words with those of Charles W. Gardner, who served as pastor to the First African Presbyterian Church in Philadelphia:

> Let me take a view of what American Slavery is. It consists in this: in making men chattels; in brutalizing the image of God, the purchase of the blood of Jesus Christ; impressing its seal on childhood, and wresting from the hand of the rightful owner that exercise of the judgment for which he is accountable only to God. It denies to the slaves, and in many parts of the country to the free colored people also, access to that heavenly chart, which is laid down by Jehovah as the only safe rule of faith and practice, the liberty of reading and understanding how he may serve God acceptably. It withholds from him all the proceeds of his labor, except a scanty subsistence, and two suits of clothing in a year, of the coarsest description.[16]

Dabney, James Henley Thornwell, Basil Manly Sr., and others spilled much ink in favor of slavery. Readers are left to wonder if, in all the spillage, they took the time to read the words of those brothers in Christ that they would have in chains.

White Man's Religion

Malcolm Little (later known as Malcolm X) was sentenced to an eight-to-ten-year stint in prison in 1946. The twenty-one-year-old had spent the last several years buried deep in a lifestyle of crime, bouncing from the Roxbury community near Boston to the streets of Harlem, dabbling in numbers running, drug deals, and burglary.

A pastor's kid, Malcolm wrote about his father's vocation:

> My two other images of my father are both outside the home. One was his role as a Baptist preacher. He never pastored in any regular church of his own; he was always a "visiting preacher." I remember especially his favorite sermon: "That little black train is a-comin' . . . an' you better get all your business right!" I guess this also fit his association with the back-to-Africa movement, with Marcus Garvey's "Black Train Homeward."

His father was a follower of Marcus Garvey who had been murdered in cold blood for daring to take a stand against white supremacy. By the time Malcolm landed in prison, the church days of his youth were long forgotten. But in the course of his time behind bars, he was able to start learning a bit of history he was never taught in school—and once he started learning, he never stopped.

"Every day now," he wrote, "the truth is coming to light."

> I never will forget how shocked I was when I began reading about slavery's total horror. It made such an impact upon me that it later became one of my favorite subjects when I became a minister of Mr. Muhammad's. The world's most monstrous crime, the sin and the blood on the white man's hands, are almost impossible to believe. Books like the one by Frederick Olmstead opened my eyes to the horrors suffered when the slave was landed in the United States.

He learned, too, about how Christianity had been used to justify the horrors of which he read. He started to connect his lived experiences of racial violence with the history lessons he imbibed, and his conclusions about Christianity became the backdrop for his eventual conversion to the Nation of Islam:

> The greatest miracle Christianity has achieved in America is that the black man in white Christian hands has not grown violent. It is a miracle that 22 million black people have not risen up against their oppressors—in which they would have been justified by all moral criteria, and even by the democratic tradition! It is a miracle that a nation of black people has so fervently continued to believe in a turn-the-other-cheek and heaven-for-you-after-you-die philosophy! It is a miracle that the American black people have remained a peaceful people, while catching all the centuries of hell that they have caught, here in white man's heaven! The miracle is that the white man's puppet Negro "leaders," his preachers and the educated Negroes laden with degrees, and others who have been allowed to wax fat off their black poor brothers, have been able to hold the black masses quiet until now.[17]

Malcolm *did* read about Nat Turner, but it was clear he saw Turner's violent quest for freedom as an anomaly within Protestant Christianity. The Christian faith, he argued, pacified Black Americans and made them roll over and accept the abuse of white men.

For all of Malcolm's reading in prison, it was still 1946. Likely, he never read the words of Daniel Payne, Charles Gardner, or Theodore Sedgewick Wright. He might not have ever read Henry Highland Garnet's electrifying sermon "Let the Monster Perish":

> Favored men, and honored of God as his instruments, speedily finish the work which he has given you to do. Emancipate,

enfranchise, educate, and give the blessings of the gospel to every American citizen.

Hear ye not how, from all high points of Time,— From peak to peak adown the mighty chain That links the ages—echoing sublime A Voice Almighty—leaps one grand refrain. Wakening the generations with a shout, And trumpet—call of thunder— Come ye out![18]

Or Garnet's pointed plea in 1843 for the enslaved of the South to rebel:

The diabolical injustice by which your liberties are cloven down, NEITHER GOD, NOR ANGELS, OR JUST MEN, COMMAND YOU TO SUFFER FOR A SINGLE MOMENT. THEREFORE IT IS YOUR SOLEMN AND IMPERATIVE DUTY TO USE EVERY MEANS, BOTH MORAL, INTEL-LECTUAL, AND PHYSICAL THAT PROMISES SUCCESS. If a band of heathen men should attempt to enslave a race of Christians, and to place their children under the influence of some false religion, surely Heaven would frown upon the men who would not resist such aggression, even to death.[19]

Indeed, Garnet's speech was so shockingly pointed in its de-nunciation of slavery and its call to arms that Frederick Doug-lass felt the need to denounce it in favor of nonviolent moral suasion.

Did Malcolm X know of the myriad Black ordained min-isters who pastored churches where they exegeted the Word of God every Sunday morning and made time to attend every anti-slavery meeting they could during the week? Did he realize these "educated Negroes laden with degrees" had been testi-fying against slavery, some of them advocating for a violent revolution to overthrow it if necessary?

Malcolm X saw Martin Luther King Jr., yes. He saw *one* Black preacher's activism, *one* loud, prominent example.

111

Did he see the cloud of witnesses who came before him? Would it have made a difference?

Africa's Christian Sons

The Protestants who first codified the laws of slavery made the mistake of seeing Christianity as synonymous with whiteness. That mistake has been repeated in this country ever since. Although Christianity started in the Middle East and made it to Africa before our Protestant forebearers even existed, the myth persisted until Malcolm X heard it from the Nation of Islam and beyond.

Thomas Oden's book *How Africa Shaped the Christian Mind* begins:

> The thesis of this book can be stated simply: Africa played a decisive role in the formation of Christian culture. Decisive intellectual achievements of Christianity were explored and understood first in Africa before they were recognized in Europe, and a millennium before they found their way to North America.[20]

He goes on to say:

> The global Christian mind has been formed out of a specific history, not out of bare-bones theoretical ideas. Much of that history occurred in Africa. Cut Africa out of the Bible and Christian memory, and you have misplaced many pivotal scenes of salvation history. It is the story of the children of Abraham in Africa; Joseph in Africa; Moses in Africa; Mary, Joseph and Jesus in Africa; and shortly thereafter after Mark and Perpetua and Athanasius and Augustine in Africa.[21]

Of course, Africa is a vast and diverse continent, not one nation, as so many early American writings make it out to be.

If you gathered the land mass of Portugal, Spain, France, Germany, Italy, Eastern Europe, the United States, India, the United Kingdom, China, and Japan together, you'd have an idea of just how *big* the continent of Africa is. Christianity did not pour across the entire continent in an equal stream.

Nevertheless, it *did* impact those whom Dabney would have most certainly categorized as "negroes" before those whom he understood as "white" ever learned the name of Jesus.

The Christian conviction of pastors like Wright, Gardner, and Payne gave them biblical language for *exactly how* slavery was wrong. It gave them biblical confidence of being made in God's image. And it gave them the biblical impetus to fight against any influence that would deny their God-given dignity.

From the ring shouts on the plantations to the staid services of Mother Bethel AME Church, Black Americans forged access to Christianity, understood it as proof that God had made them equal to their white counterparts. Whether that meant arming for a rebellion, preaching at an anti-slavery convention, or going about the quiet resistance of refusing to let religious persecution keep them from worshiping, Black Americans fought to be recognized as the image bearers that they were and are.

6

"Slavery Has Well Nigh Murdered Him"

Charlotte Forten was a church girl who turned that teaching into her life's mission. She is the culmination of so much of what we've discussed already—she is the granddaughter of James Forten, she sat under Daniel Payne's preaching, and she married a Presbyterian minister who followed in Theodore Sedgewick Wright's Princeton footsteps. She inherited the rich legacy of her abolitionist, feminist aunts and represents the changing tide of America. And she was a force in her own right, her flash point being the capture of fugitive slave Anthony Burns.

America's landscape was changing.

In 1845, the term *Manifest Destiny* was coined to describe the clarion call of the day: westward expansion. Every few years, new states were added to the union through war and compromise. The transatlantic slave trade had long since come to an end. Southern slaveholders were keen to protect the property of their "peculiar institution" at all costs. The Northern states had either done away with slavery outright or had enacted gradual abolition.

Two distinct worldviews began to emerge. In the North, industrialism clamored for progress that relied on cheap labor. In the South, agrarianism rested squarely on the shoulders of the four million Africans who lived in captivity. The two regions might have continued their standoff in a stalemate were it not for one fact: the South was hemorrhaging slaves.

Every day, a new poster advertised a reward for the recapture of a runaway slave. Every day, Northern abolitionists found ways to aid these refugees in their quest toward freedom. And every day, the Southern powers that be grew more anxious about the uncertain future of the slaveholder's lifestyle.

In 1851, the exodus from the South would become so frequent that Dr. Samuel Cartwright studied *why* the enslaved were trying to escape in droves. His research eventually led him to declare the discovery of a new disease: *drapetomania*. In his book *Diseases and Peculiarities of the Negro Race*, Cartwright explained that the disease was "well known to our planters and overseers." Its symptoms? "It induces the negro to run away from service" and "is as much a disease of the mind as any other species of mental alienation, and much more curable, as a general rule."

Never fear, argued Cartwright! "With the advantages of proper medical advice, strictly followed, this troublesome practice that many negroes have of running away, can be almost entirely prevented."

The disease thrived, he argued, when masters were either too permissive or too cruel with the enslaved. The permissiveness came when

the white man attempts to oppose the Deity's will, by trying to make the negro anything else than "the submissive knee-

116

bender," (which the Almighty declared he should be,) by trying to raise him to a level with himself, or by putting himself on an equality with the negro.[1]

And the cruelty, he said, could be avoided by treating the enslaved the way the good Lord intended: treat them well, but not well enough that they think of themselves as equals. And "if any one of more of them, at any time, are inclined to raise their heads to a level with their master or overseer," they should be punished and sent back to the "submissive state" God intended them to occupy for all of time.[2]

Historians have debated over whether or not this was a serious medical analysis or a tongue-in-cheek advice column, but either way, it spoke to the mounting tensions of Southern slaveholders keen to hold on to their property.

If the desire to escape enslavement was a disease, many Southerners saw Northern abolitionists as the source of the outbreak, especially since most runaways escaped from the Southern states that bordered free states.

In 1852, South Carolina started whispering her first intentions of seceding, and in 1860, the state's declaration of secession pointed at abolitionists as the basis for its decision. The state argued that the North denounced slavery as sinful, established slave societies, and encouraged the enslaved to run away, a trifecta that typified the upbringing of Charlotte Forten.

A Changing Landscape

Charlotte was only thirteen when news of the Fugitive Slave Act spread like wildfire through her Pennsylvania home. The only daughter of Robert Bridges Forten (son of James, brother of Margaretta, Harriet, and Sarah) and his first wife, Charlotte lost her mother when she was only three. Her father had since remarried, and Charlotte (Lottie, as she was called) spent most of her time at 95 Lombard Street, where she would eventually live with her grandmother and a loving assortment of aunts and uncles. Her favorite was Aunt Margaretta, who never had any children of her own and doted on Lottie and the young girl's education.

Under Margaretta's tutelage, the young girl would have been well aware of the news rippling through the so-called city of brotherly love. Henry Clay, the blustering senator from Kentucky, had proposed a fugitive slave law as part of a compromise meant to quell the South's fury at the North's reticence to help return fugitive slaves.

The Fugitive Slave Act would ultimately make the Northern states responsible for returning runaways to their enslavers in the South. If Northerners didn't comply with this new law, they would be heavily fined and forced to serve prison time.

Nevertheless, the Fortens and their in-laws, the Purvises, still maintained a very important role in the Underground Railroad. Lottie's aunt Harriet and her husband, Robert, were a stop on the railroad in Pennsylvania, and what money the Fortens maintained after James's death was still used to aid the abolitionist cause.

If the deeds of Lottie's family ever came to light, they would all be transgressors of the law, starting with her grandfather, James Forten. The sail-making magnate and abolitionist died when Charlotte was seven, but he left an indelible mark on his family. His children eagerly followed in his footsteps.

Margaretta, the oldest aunt, took over as family matriarch after her father died, hosting dinners for the likes of William Lloyd Garrison and Wendell Phillips. Robert Purvis, husband of the second-oldest Forten aunt, Harriet, shared the title of Father of the Underground Railroad with family friend William Still. His and Harriet's home was a haven through which countless refugees had passed from the enslaved South to

Philadelphia, New York, Boston, and Canada. Lottie's third-oldest aunt, Sarah Louisa, had spent her youth writing fiery rebuttals of slavery for *The Liberator*.

Charlotte's own father had spoken at the Female Anti-Slavery Society and would eventually join the Union army at the age of fifty-one, even though no Forten had been enslaved since James's grandfather.

Lottie herself was normally a bystander to the hustle and bustle of 95 Lombard Street. She watched as her aunts attended anti-slavery meetings, wrote fiery abolitionist poetry and prose, networked with their associates to help get refugees to safety, and within the safety of those Lombard Street walls, rested their shoulders from the exhaustion of pushing the anti-slavery cause.

She witnessed them shed tears over the fate of Southern refugees forced to run away from everything they knew, even their own children, to be free. She listened as they raged over families who ran north to avoid separation at slave auctions in the South only to suffer the same fate thanks to this cruel new law of the North. She felt the squeeze of her own heart when she heard of free Black people far less privileged being kidnapped and taken south if they fit the description of a runaway slave.

Purvis's family friend, Harriet Jacobs, described the scene in Boston in particular agony:

> Many families, who had lived in the city for twenty years, fled from it now. Many a poor washerwoman, who, by hard labor, had made herself a comfortable home, was obliged to sacrifice her furniture, bid a hurried farewell to friends, and seek her fortune among strangers in Canada. Many a wife discovered a secret she had never known before—that her husband was a fugitive, and must leave her to insure his own safety. Worse still, many a husband discovered that his wife had fled from slavery years ago, and as "the child follows the condition of its mother," the children of his love were liable to be seized and

119

carried into slavery. Every where, in those humble homes, there was consternation and anguish. But what cared the legislators of the "dominant race" for the blood they were crushing out of trampled hearts?[3]

The Fallout of a New Law

At thirteen, Charlotte's entire world began to take on a new form. Though the North had not been a haven for all runaways— George Washington himself had hunted for his runaway Ona Judge until the day he died—it held some hope of refuge. Now, even white Northerners who were merely apathetic toward the plight of the enslaved would be forced to link arms with slave catchers.

Family friends who were fugitive slaves packed up their bags and left, heading toward safety in Canada. Abolitionists the Fortens knew and worked with were thrown into prison for helping fugitives escape. Children enrolled in her aunt Margaretta's school disappeared, never to be seen or heard from again.

In the years following the Fugitive Slave Act, Charlotte's family continued to aid fugitives. Uncle Robert Purvis became even more outspoken about the injustice of slavery, and the Garrisons were more frequent house guests. Her own father immigrated to Canada with his second family, sick over the mounting hostilities in the States. The revolving door on Lombard Street welcomed cousins, aunts, and uncles as Lottie became a more permanent guest until a letter from her father informed her of a connection he'd made for her in Salem, Massachusetts.

Lottie was seventeen when she left the house on Lombard Street. She was warmly welcomed by the Remonds of Salem, a family of Black abolitionists whose pedigree was also a force to reckon with. They had taken the local public schools to task, advocating that their children be schooled right alongside the city's white children, receiving the same caliber of education.

Like Philadelphia, Salem had a thriving Black community. The small town was only forty minutes from Boston, where the Fugitive Slave Law had brought the life of a young runaway crashing down around him.

Anthony Burns was just a few years older than Charlotte (born in 1834), but where Charlotte had grown up in freedom and relative privilege in Philadelphia, Anthony had been born into slavery in Virginia. He was not quite twenty when he escaped to Boston, only to be arrested on trumped-up burglary charges and held until his master could claim him.

Lottie and her schoolmates would have been aware of Anthony Burns's impending trial that summer of 1854. She would have heard about the five thousand people who listened at Faneuil Hall while several abolitionists railed against the illegality

121

of forcing a free state to do a slave state's bidding. Ironically, in some of the very same rhetoric the Southerners would later use to defend secession, listeners at the meeting were urged to put Massachusetts law above the national law, relying on the state's right to decide whether or not it would become a bedfellow of the enslavers.

Lottie would have also known about the hundreds of white abolitionists who rioted outside the courthouse and the handful of Black abolitionists who tried to break in and rescue Anthony, some going so far as to use a battering ram to knock down the front door.

She watched and waited, along with the rest of the country, to see how the Fugitive Slave Act would play out amid the outcry of Bostonians who didn't want to see their city turned into a battleground for slaveholders.

She watched and waited, along with her family back in Philadelphia, to see just how effective the fiery sermons of the abolitionists would be when judge and jury's hands were tied by federal law.

She watched and waited, along with so many other young Black Americans, to see if the young man their age would be remanded back into a life of enslavement.

When the news came, it devastated the young woman.

To-day Massachusetts has again been disgraced; again she has showed her submission to the Slave Power; and Oh! With what deep sorrow do we think of what will doubtless be the fate of that poor man, when he is again consigned to the horrors of slavery. With what scorn must that government be regarded which cowardly assembles thousands of soldiers to satisfy the demands of slaveholders; to deprive of his freedom a man, created in God's own image, whose sole offense is the color of his skin! And if resistance is offered to this outrage, these soldiers are to shoot down American citizens without mercy; and this by express orders of a government which proudly boasts of being the freest in the world; this on the very soil where the Revolution of 1776 began; in sight of the battlefield, where thousands of brave men fought and died in opposing British tyranny, which was nothing compared with the American oppression of today.[4]

The letter of the law required his transport back to Virginia, but, she thought, the *spirit* of the American promise required his immediate freedom from enslavement. Perhaps she was one of the 50,000 people who gathered in the streets of Boston to watch the young man marched back to his Southern doom. Maybe she saw the sixteen hundred men who kept the crowd in check as Anthony was taken aboard the ship that would take him back to slavery. Possibly, she donated what little money she had to contribute to the eventual purchase of his freedom one year later.

Regardless, this was one of many brushes Charlotte would have with Slave Power,[5] as it was dubbed by abolitionists, in her long and fruitful life. Her journal spanned the next thirty-eight years of her life, as would her fight for African Americans to be seen as being made in God's glorious image.

The Might of Slave Power

Lottie didn't name a single authority responsible for Anthony's imprisonment. Instead, she lambasted the entire government for its "cowardly" decision.

Charlotte was a devoted Christian her entire life.[6] She would end up married to Francis James Grimké, the long-term pastor of Fifteenth Street Presbyterian Church in DC, and spend part of her career devoted to both practical and religious education.

Charlotte was familiar with the following passage in Ephesians:

Finally, be strong in the Lord and in the strength of his might. Put on the whole armor of God, that you may be able to stand against the schemes of the devil. For we do not wrestle against flesh and blood, but against the rulers, against the authorities, against the cosmic powers over this present darkness, against the spiritual forces of evil in the heavenly places. (6:10–12 ESV)

So often, reflections on America's history of slavery are reduced to debates about practicality. Did the North win because of her industrial prowess? How would the Southern economy survive without slavery? How would the Union survive without thirteen of her states?

It can be reduced to a matter of legality. Was the North legally required to extradite refugees? Were Southern states constitutionally allowed to secede? Did Black American citizens have rights the North was required to respect?

But with this May 1854 passage in her journal, Charlotte displays a different perspective. Has slavery derived its power from practicality or legality? Or from cosmic powers, present darkness, and the spiritual forces of evil?

Charlotte Forten Grimké

Lottie's words might inappropriately be dismissed as the immature ravings of a young girl too naïve to understand the money driving the fight over slavery's expansion.

Lottie could have never known that her journals would one day be an important piece of Americana, offering incredible insight to American life before, during, and after the Civil War. She did not anticipate becoming a folklorist as she journaled in the solitude of her own bedroom at the Remond house or later when she wrote of her experience teaching emancipated citizens in South Carolina's Sea Islands.

She was writing in the solitude of her own bedroom at the Remond home, not for the annals of history.

Yet history received those words, and in case anyone doubted the force of the Slave Power she referenced, she gave further insight into it in the very next entry.

It was Sunday when Charlotte next sat before her journal. As she reflected on the beauty of a new day, she mourned,

> How strange it is that in a world so beautiful, there can be so much wickedness on this delightful day, while many are enjoying themselves in their happy homes, not poor Burns only, but millions besides are suffering in chains; how many Christian ministers today will mention him, or those who suffer with him? How many will speak from the pulpit against the cruel outrage on humanity which has just been committed, or against the many, even worse ones, which are committed in this country every day? Too well do we know that there are but few, and these few alone deserve to be called ministers of Christ, whose doctrine was "Break every yoke, and let the oppressed go free."[7]

"There are but few" Christian ministers, Charlotte said, who would speak out against the injustice of slavery. There were but few Christian ministers who would understand the need to denounce Slave Power. In absolute frustration, Charlotte labeled men who failed to recognize the incredible sin of slavery and the need to denounce Slave Power as undeserving of being called ministers of Christ.

Many American ministers, particularly in the South, were not living in ignorance about the realities of slavery in their country. Rather, they were *devout apologists* for the enterprise.

In 1851, Robert Lewis Dabney wrote a letter outlining his opinion on the morality of slavery. In it, he argued that "this foreign and semi-barbarous population" had arrived in America, not by the doing of the present generation, but by enslavers of the past. As such, the South was making do with the

15th Street Presbyterian Church, where Francis James Grimké was long-time pastor

Black population (which he likened to the plague of frogs in Egypt) the best way they could. "The remedy," Dabney wrote, "is slavery."

A man who saw slavery so very differently than so many of the Black ministers discussed here—who held disdain for Black Americans until the day he died—spent most of his ministry studying, teaching, and defending the Bible.

How?

The answers vary. White supremacy ravaged America (and in so many ways, defined it) from its founding. But if the Christians among these pages used the Bible to argue that African Americans were made in the image of God and endowed with identity, dignity, and significance as a result, how could a Christian who read the same Bible arrive at such a different conclusion?

Slave Power was so much more than the rantings of a teenage girl. Lottie understood this discussion was far more complex than book, chapter, and verse. It was a clash between image bearers and principalities, an issue fought first in the battleground of the human heart.

Murdering the *Imago Dei*

Another pastor, William Watkins, begged to differ with Dabney. He used his newspaper to critique those who would enslave others—and to cry out on behalf of Anthony Burns:

> Slavery is murder in the highest degree. Every slaveholder is a murderer, a wholesale murderer. Those who apologise for them are worse than murderers. If one of these midnight and noonday assassins were to rush into the house of a white man, and strive to bind him hand and foot, and tear God's image from his brow, and be shot in the attempt, no one would characterize that act as murder. Not at all. It would be considered an act of righteous retribution. The man who sent a bullet through the tyrant's heart would be almost extravagantly lauded. This would be done, we remark, if the man to be enslaved, or murdered, which is the same thing, were a white man. Now take the following case. A colored man is living quietly in Boston, one mile from the Bunker Hill Monument. **He is a free man, for God created him. He stamped his image upon him. Slavery has well nigh murdered him.**[8]

Watkins was uncle to Frances Ellen Watkins Harper, writer, teacher, activist, and Renaissance woman. Frances grew up with her uncle after the death of her parents, learning in his school and sitting under his tutelage as he decried the slavery of the land. She would become as adept as he was at critiquing the horrors of American chattel slavery.

Reverend Watkins's use of the word *murder* might have struck listeners outside of his antislavery circle as a little dramatic—

particularly when talking about the time-honored American tradition of chattel slavery. But Watkins's point was an important one for his listeners to heed: if mankind is made in the image of God, then reducing that image to dollars and cents— stripping that image of its individual identity, significance, and worth—was, indeed, a type of murder.

Lottie didn't know that her entry after the extradition of Anthony Burns in the summer of 1854 could resonate with modern readers who watched injustice rage during the week, wondering if it would be addressed in the pulpit on Sunday: "How many Christian ministers will mention him or those who suffer with him?"

Her question would speak to believers sitting in their seats on Sunday, hearts aching from a salacious headline that feels altogether horrifying and familiar. They would incline toward the pulpit during the pastoral prayer, holding a collective breath and wondering if the man charged with shepherding their flock would mention the soul-deep wounds of some of his sheep.

Like Charlotte, so many Christians are met with silence.

But young Lottie didn't give up in the face of Slave Power. She looked the dragon in the eye, fully aware it would take much more than one woman's efforts to slay. Rather than discounting Christianity altogether, she agreed with abolitionist John Brown that many theologically astute Christians still weren't up to snuff when it came to the ABCs of the gospel.

Put another way: Robert L. Dabney could argue abstract biblical principles with the best of them, but he still didn't understand how to respect the *imago Dei* in others. First Corinthians 13 comes to mind: "If I speak in the tongues of men and of angels, but have not love, I am only a resounding gong or a clanging cymbal" (v. 1 NIV). Lottie did not discount Christianity entirely; she discounted a version of it that was unfaithful to the principles of the love Christ called his people to (John 13:35).

The War Wages On

Charlotte's fight against Slave Power was not confined to the pages of her journal. At the age of twenty-five, in the heat of the Civil War, she traveled to the Sea Islands of South Carolina to become a missionary teacher to the newly emancipated African Americans there. Charlotte was the only Black teacher on the island, the only Black woman there who had not been formerly enslaved, and often the only person who was neither formerly enslaved nor a white Union soldier.

After her stint in South Carolina, she taught in a few other schools before settling in Washington, DC, where she married Francis James Grimké. Unlike Charlotte, Francis was a formerly enslaved man whose own white relatives had kept him in captivity when his slaveholding father died. But very much like Charlotte, he took part in the legacy of abolition that had been brewing in cities like DC, Philadelphia, and Boston for years.

In 1918, four years after Charlotte died, the widower preached a Christmas Eve sermon inspired by yet another war. Like the younger Lottie, he lamented that America had "little or no interest in true democracy, in its rights of man as man,"[9] as evidenced by the way that the country treated people made in the image of God.

Charlotte married the type of Christian she had prayed would occupy more and more pulpits in America. And even after the abolishment of the slavery that had held him captive, Francis understood that America had a long way to go in fully embracing the inherent dignity of man. He spoke with a fierceness that would have made his late wife proud.

> I believe there is going to be developed a higher type of Christianity than at present prevail than the miserable apology that now goes under that name. Things are as they are today in these great nations of the world, and it has fared with these weaker and darker races and nations as it has, because the so

129

called Church of God has been recreant to its high trust; has been dominated by such a cowardly and worldly spirit that it has always been willing to listen to the voice of man instead of the voice of God.[10]

Like Lottie, Francis understood that Christianity was not defined by those who failed to recognize the simple notion that the entirety of the human race merits respect. He understood that the racial prejudice that defined so many professing Christians in America did not define Jesus.

Francis James Grimké wrote these words at the height of the Great War, a conflict that brought Black soldiers face-to-face with the hypocrisy of the white sons of America. He wrote them while President Woodrow Wilson, who would screen *Birth of a Nation* at the White House and laud it as accurate history, occupied the highest seat in the nation.

Wilson had run on a platform that, while not overtly reconciliatory toward Black Americans, promised progress that they could get behind. Once he was elected, though, he brought segregation into the highest offices in America, separating political workers who had once sat side by side. He converted back to the "good old boy" politics his Southern roots were most comfortable embracing.

Grimké wrote to Wilson himself, championing the rights that the president had once promised:

The simple fact is, the only hope which the colored man has of fair treatment in this country, is to be found in men, who like yourself, believe in God and in his Son, Jesus Christ, and who feel that the greatest service they can render to their fellow men is to square their lives with the principles of the Christian religion, and to bear about with them ever the noble and beautiful spirit of the Man of Nazareth. With a man of your known Christian character at the head of affairs, I am sure that the race with which I am identified will have no just grounds for complaint. It is a comforting thought, especially, to those who are struggling against great odds, to know that the God of Abraham, of Isaac, and of Jacob—the God that the Bible reveals, is on the throne, and that under Him, as His viceregent, will be a man who has the courage of his convictions, and who will not falter where duty calls. You have my best wishes, and the earnest prayer that you may be guided by Divine wisdom in the arduous duties and responsibilities that are so soon to devolve upon you as the Chief Executive of this great nation.[11]

Wilson would fail Grimké and so many other Black Americans, even as he professed to serve the same God and the same cause. His presidency would coincide with World War I, The Great Migration, and Red Summer, a time of increased racial hostility and violence across the entire country as Black men and women continued to seek the rights their nation had promised them.

Moving back again to June of 1854 when America was on the cusp of the Civil War, the laws in place protected slaveholders' rights to their property rather than the inalienable rights of the enslaved. As a teenaged girl, Charlotte Forten understood what so many grown men would spend the next several years of the bloody conflict denying: that God has already had the last word on who is deserving of respect and whose rights are worthy of being fought for and protected. And even though these words were written in her private journal, they echo throughout history. Joining forces with so many other powerful voices, her words proclaim the unwavering truth that image bearers in the so-called freest nation in the world were deserving of so much more than what they were being given by the country they called home.

7

Frater-Feeling

There was no *one* kind of abolitionist. While it may be tempting to create a neat and tidy narrative to centralize the rallying cry, this is not one simple, straightforward story of activism. It's also important to discuss some of the disagreements abolitionists had with each other about defending the *imago Dei*.

Twenty-six-year-old Mary Ann Shadd sat down to write a letter.

Most likely, she picked up her pen at the end of a long day of teaching in one of New York's underfunded Black schools. As a Black female teacher, her income was doubly impacted— her meager earnings were not enough to support herself or offer aid to the floundering basement school. Her room was modest, particularly compared to her relatively comfortable upbringing.

Mary Ann had been born into a middle-class abolitionist family in Delaware. When the state outlawed the education of Black students, the Shadds had the means to pick up and move

Library and Archives Canada

Mary Ann Shadd and her newspaper, the *Provincial Freeman*

to Pennsylvania and pursue educational opportunities there. After training as a teacher, Mary Ann worked in a handful of New England schools before settling in New York, one of the most inhospitable Northern cities for Black education.

The young woman came by her abolitionist fire honestly. Her childhood home had often been a hub for the Underground Railroad. She had seen the horrors of Southern slavery through the eyes of the weary travelers who fled it and watched her parents provide sanctuary to fellow image bearers who risked their lives to run north.

In 1848, Frederick Douglass asked the readers of his newspaper, the *North Star*, what could be done to improve the plight of Black Americans. Mary Ann—full of firsthand knowledge of the work of abolition—had answers aplenty.

> We have been holding conventions for years—have been assembling together and whining over our difficulties and afflictions, passing resolutions on resolutions to any extent; but it does really seem that we have made but little progress, considering our resolves. . . . We should do more and talk less.[1]

And who were the people Mary Ann saw doing the least? The clergy.

The ministers assume to be instructors in every matter, a thing we would not object to, provided they taught, even in accordance with the age; but in our literature, they hang tenaciously to exploded customs (as if we were not creatures of progress as well as others), as they do in everything else. The course of some of our high priests, makes your humble servant, and many others, think money, and not the good of the people, is at the bottom.[2]

National Portrait Gallery, Smithsonian Institution

Henry Highland Garnet

The clergyman who stirred Mary Ann to pen these assertions was none other than Reverend Henry Highland Garnet, whose radical call for rebellion had caused the widespread pearl-clutching of many an abolitionist—Frederick Douglass included.

Abolitionist Infighting

Abolitionists utilized the *imago Dei* to argue against slavery and for the rights of Black Americans, but they did not always get along while doing so. In fact, some disagreements grew so heated and the rivalries so fraught that history sometimes focuses only on the perceived victors of the struggle.

Most history books will not include Garnet's fiery sermon "Let the Monster Perish," but one would be hard-pressed to find a history book lacking the key details of Frederick Douglass's life and activism.

Douglass and Garnet were openly at odds on more than one occasion. When Garnet issued his famous 1843 call to rebellion to the slaves of the South, Douglass publicly distanced himself from such radicalism. Douglass believed in a nonviolent approach to abolition, whereas Garnet (like Walker and Turner before him) preached resistance by any means necessary.

A few months after Mary Ann leveled her criticism at Garnet for a heavenly mindedness that kept him from being of much earthly good, Garnet sent Douglass a letter that included these lines:

You did not even want to know whether I was going to that country before you labored like a Hercules to blacken my character in the eyes of a people who may never see me. I knew, sir, that you in your hot pursuit after worthless, and a transient fame, you would ever sink so low, that you would have to reach up, standing on tiptoe, to find the level of meanness where common knaves are inclined to pause. Ah, sir, the green-eyed monster has made you mad. Pardon me, when I tell you that you never imbibed a spirit so narrow from any dark son of Maryland, living or dead. But why should I marvel? When did you ever manifest friendship to any colored man who differed from you in sentiment?[3]

The letter was published by the Maryland arm of the American Colonization Society in their journal (*Maryland Colonization Journal*), as salacious proof that abolitionists did not know how to get along:

Considering the intense sympathy manifested for the slaves by Abolitionists, it is a matter of astonishment that so little frater-feeling exists between these philanthropists for each other. From all quarters we hear of strife and wranglings. Not only between the whites, where it might reasonably be expected, but between the colored leaders themselves. As a specimen of this interchange of "Friendship's offerings," we copy a letter from the Rev. H. H. Garnet, a coloured man of

education and talents, to his brother and fellow-laborer Frederick Douglass. It is one of the most able and most courteous of
the class we have seen. It seems this being *lionized* in England
causes no little jealousy and heart-burning among our coloured
adventurers.[4]

The bickering between Douglass and Garnet provided just
the kind of spectacle the Maryland Colonization Society loved
to place in their monthly newspaper to show the disorganized
goals of the abolitionist movement.

But while abolitionists like Frederick Douglass and the late
James Forten lambasted the goals of the American Colonization Society, Bethel AME Church presented R. J. Breckinridge
with a gold snuff box in gratitude for his "work to prevent
legislation that would place restrictions on slaveholders' ability to manumit slaves and the rights of the state's free black
population."[5] And back when James Forten first criticized
the American Colonization Society, he also supported his
longtime friend Paul Cuffe in one of America's first "back to
Africa" movements. By the time the wealthy Black sea captain died in 1817, many formerly enslaved people had taken
advantage of the ACS's free passage to Liberia, despite some
of the society's more racist leanings. (You may recall some
of the quotes about Black inequality from ACS members in
chapter 2.)

What If I Am a Woman?

There have been many names mentioned throughout the story
of conscientious abolitionism—particularly Black preachers:
Henry Highland Garnet, Henry McNeal Turner, Charles W.
Gardner, Daniel Payne, Theodore Sedgwick Wright, Richard
Allen, and others.

Notably, there are no women on that list.

And during chapter 3's discussion of Black women activists, Black female preachers were notably absent.

This is by design—not to downplay the significance of Black women preachers, but to situate it here amid the disagreements facing Black abolitionists.

Often, abolitionists had issues seeing women in any sort of lectern, whether preaching a sermon or advocating for the rights of their fellow human beings. When Maria Stewart delivered her second speech in 1832, she became the first American woman— Black or white—to speak publicly to a mixed crowd. While some fell mesmerized by the sound of her voice and the force of her fervor, much of the feedback Stewart received was negative.

It wasn't Stewart's words themselves but the fact that she was a woman speaking those words. In a time when women were supposed to exercise their morality behind the closed doors of their homes, Stewart's authoritative speeches were jarring to many of her hearers.

As such, her womanhood was often a fixture of her public speeches:

Methinks I heard a spiritual interrogation—"Who shall go forward, and take off the reproach that is cast upon the people of color? Shall it be a woman?" And my heart made this reply—"If it is thy will, be it even so, Lord Jesus!"[6]

O, woman, woman, upon you I call; for upon your exertions almost entirely depends whether the rising generation shall be anything more than we have been or not. O, woman, woman, your example is powerful, your influence great; it extends over your husbands and over your children, and throughout the circle of your acquaintance.[7]

But it was her 1833 farewell speech when Stewart got to the heart of her passion for speaking out, not just about racial injustice, but about the Word of God. After giving her testimony, Stewart declared:

> What if I am a woman; is not the God of ancient times the God of these modern days? Did he not raise up Deborah to be a mother and a judge in Israel? Did not Queen Esther save the lives of the Jews? And Mary Magdalene first declare the resurrection of Christ from the dead? Come, said the woman of Samaria, and see a man that hath told me all things that ever I did; is not this the Christ? St. Paul declared that it was a shame for a woman to speak in public, yet our great High Priest and Advocate did not condemn the woman for a more notorious offense than this; neither will he condemn this worthless worm. The bruised reed he will not break, and the smoking flax he will not quench till he send forth judgment unto victory. Did St. Paul but know of our wrongs and deprivations, I presume he would make no objection to our pleading in public for our rights.[8]

Stewart echoed the argument of Jarena Lee, the first woman preacher in the African Methodist Episcopal Church and ten years into her itinerate preaching ministry by the time of Stewart's first public appearance in 1832. When Lee first approached Richard Allen—founder of the African Methodist Episcopal Church—to share with him her sense that God was calling her to preach, he denied her.

Lee recalls in her memoir:

> If the man may preach, because the Saviour died for him, why not the woman? seeing he died for her also. Is he not a whole Saviour, instead of a half one? as those who hold it wrong for a woman to preach, would seem to make it appear. Did not Mary first preach the risen Saviour, and is not the doctrine of the resurrection the very climax of Christianity—hangs not all our hope on this, as argued by St. Paul? Then did not Mary, a

woman, preach the gospel? for she preached the resurrection of the crucified Son of God.

Anticipating the denial of her reader, Lee says:

But some will say that Mary did not expound the Scripture, therefore, she did not preach, in the proper sense of the term. To this I reply, it may be that the term preach in those primitive times, did not mean exactly what it is now made to mean; perhaps it was a great deal more simple then, than it is now—if it were not, the unlearned fishermen could not have preached the gospel at all, as they had no learning.[9]

Lee wore Allen down indirectly.

One day, while sitting in a church service listening to a man's

MRS JARENA LEE.
Preacher of the A. M. E. Church.

stumbling sermon, clearly inept at the task before him, Lee stood up and took over. She testified of God's Word so articulately that Allen determined she *must* have been called by God.

Contrast this with Reverend Samuel Eli Cornish, Presbyterian minister and the founder of the very first Black newspaper, the *Freedman's Journal.* Cornish felt that the education of Black women was of supreme importance, writing that "every measure for the thorough and proper education of [black] females is a blow aimed directly at slavery."

He also agreed with abolitionist Charles B. Ray, who noted in the *Colored American* in 1837,

Daughters are destined to be wives and mothers—they should, therefore, be taught to know how to manage a house and govern and instruct children. Without this knowledge, they would be lost, and as mothers distracted, their homes would be in disorder, and their children would grow up loose and without character.

Feminist thinker though he was, Frederick Douglass's thoughts lined up with both Cornish's and Ray's: "a well-regulated household, in every station of society, is one of woman's brightest ornaments."

It came as no surprise to anyone when Reverend Cornish expressed concern regarding "some of America's virtuous and talented daughters" pursuing "masculine views and measures":

> We are anxious that woman, lovely woman, should fill the whole of her important and truly elevated sphere. Let not an iota be taken from her influence, or curtailed from her appropriate efforts. Woman was created to be the "help-meet" and not the idol or slave of man; and in everything truly virtuous and noble, she is furnished by our bountiful Creator, with all the intellectual, moral, and physical requisites for her important place.[10]

In the fashion of an articulate newspaperman, Cornish couched his disapproval of women as public activists in the language of virtue and nobility, careful to place conditions on their effort. Fellow Presbyterian minister J. W. C. Pennington spoke much more forcefully in his essay "Licensing Women to Preach":

> In every sphere of labor, physical and moral, Providence seems to have appropriated the proper laborers. In agricultural labor all the heavy work is assigned to the man, because he is physically best constituted for it. The same in all mechanical labor. In the army, in the navy, in mercantile employment, and in all the learned professions where mighty thought and laborious

investigation are needed, the man, strong in body and mind, is fitted by nature to execute what the weaker sex is incapacitated for, both physically and mentally. Must the Church, that needs the most manly strength, the most gigantic minds to execute her labors, confide them to those whom nature has fitted for the easier toils of life? Shall the labors of a Paul, a Silas, a Peter, a Luther, a Calvin, a Wesley, be trusted to the weaker sex? Shall the mighty monuments of the translations and commentations of the Scriptures, and historical investigations of truth, be committed to her who is clearly designed by the Creator to labors less, much less, in exercise and exertion of body and mind? Has this ever been the case? No, verily.[11]

Pennington was himself a fugitive slave and an ardent defender of the *imago Dei*. And yet, he disagreed with the likes of Jarena Lee about how the doctrine should be lived out in womanhood and manhood. Samuel Eli Cornish published an entire newspaper defending the *imago Dei* by critiquing enslavement and injustice. Still, he and Maria Stewart disagreed over how the biblical teaching applied to women defending those same rights.

A full treatment of the church's historical ideas about women preachers and teachers is outside of the scope of this book, but it is important to note that the *very same issue* being discussed in present day divided abolitionists almost two hundred years ago.

Women's Suffrage or Black Suffrage

Even after emancipation, activists continued to disagree on the way forward for Black rights and dignity. Sojourner Truth, Frances Ellen Watkins Harper, and Frederick Douglass split over the issue of suffrage. Sojourner advocated for universal suffrage—for Black men *and* women.

Harper and Douglass were both members of the American Equal Rights Association. Once slavery ended, the two activists faced the question of whether Black men would get to vote before women. Some factions prioritized white female suffrage; others, Black male suffrage; still others did not want *any* suffrage unless *everyone* was allowed the right to vote.

Douglass was focused on Black men's suffrage before women's:

> It may be asked, "Why do you want it? Some men have got along very well without it. Women have not this right." Shall we justify one wrong by another? This is the sufficient answer. Shall we at this moment justify the deprivation of the Negro of the right to vote, because some one else is deprived of that privilege? I hold that women, as well as men, have the right to vote [Applause.], and my heart and voice go with the movement to extend suffrage to woman; but that question rests upon another basis than which our right rests.[12]

Douglass was a proponent of women's suffrage—he had been a longtime friend of suffragette Susan B. Anthony—but when it came to who could access the ballot first (Black men or white women), he reasoned that since *men* already had the right to vote in America, *Black* men's inclusion should be a given.

Frances Ellen Watkins Harper recognized that the suffrage movement in which Douglass was entrenched bore a greater concern with the rights of white women than Black women. In her famous 1866 speech "We Are All Bound Up Together," she stated:

> You white women speak here of rights. I speak of wrongs. I, as a colored woman, have had in this country an education which has made me feel as if I were in the situation of Ishmael, my hand against every man, and every man's hand against me.

Predicting white feminist backlash against Douglass's suffrage priorities, she went on to say:

> While there exists this brutal element in society which tramples upon the feeble and treads down the weak, I tell you that if there

143

is any class of people who need to be lifted out of their airy nothings and selfishness, it is the white women of America.[13]

Sojourner Truth shares Harper's sentiments in her own speech:

There is a great stir about colored men getting their rights, but not a word about the colored women; and if colored men get their rights, and not colored women theirs, you see the colored men will be masters over the women, and it will be just as bad as it was before. So I am for keeping the thing going while things are stirring; because if we wait till it is still, it will take a great while to get it going again.[14]

In the end, Douglass got his wish, and Black men were afforded the right to vote while women had to wait until the twentieth century to enjoy that same right. As a result, the American Equal Rights Association dissolved, as did some of the relationships therein.

Frederick Douglass made incredible strides for the rights of Black Americans, and would continue to do so, but Harper and Truth felt those strides were incomplete without special consideration to the rights of Black women, who had been fighting tooth and nail for centuries.

To Emigrate or Not to Emigrate

Mary Ann Shadd would have been decidedly in Maria Stewart's corner on the matter of women and public speaking. Whether she would have agreed with the ordination of Jarena Lee is a bit more questionable, simply because she was famously suspicious of all clergy. Fiery sermons were not enough. She wanted action.

For her, that action culminated in moving to Canada shortly after the Fugitive Slave Law of 1850 was enacted. Black Americans—both the fugitive, the freeborn, and the freed alike—saw the terror of such legislation in the threat of recapture and mistaken identity. While many Americans felt called to stay and fight for their rightful place in the country of their birth, Mary Ann was one of many who decided emigration was a viable option to procure Black rights.

So while Henry Highland Garnet and others stayed behind in America doing, in Mary Ann Shadd's opinion, a whole lot of nothing, she packed up and went to Canada to do *something*.

That *something* became an integrated school in Canada and the launch of a yearslong campaign aimed at convincing Black Americans to immigrate to a country where she felt they could achieve the level of respect they had been grasping for in America.

Mary Ann was not the first Black activist to espouse this cause. Remember, Paul Cuffe—the wealthy sea captain and longtime friend of James Forten—was a vocal advocate for emigration back to Africa before the movement by the same name was made famous some years later. He saw a colony in Africa as a way for Black Americans to prove they could foster economic stability and success in their homeland, much like Cuffe himself had done in America.

Cuffe's visions of setting up a colony in Sierra Leone were ultimately thwarted by the founding of the American Colonization Society.

But when the American Colonization Society was founded as a sort of unholy alliance of missionaries and Southern slaveholders, Cuffe's friends, the Philadelphia blacks, immediately saw

145

it as a scheme to get rid of free blacks to make slavery more secure. Forten's letter informing Cuffe of the black defection from colonization may have arrived in time to contribute to the heart attack from which Cuffe did not recover. After his death the American Colonization Society used Cuffe for its propaganda. This did not help Cuffe's reputation with most American blacks, but those who went out to found Liberia—often with the stated aim of civilizing and converting Africa—found Cuffe's colonists happy, were welcomed by Cuffe's friends, and everyone had much good to say of him.[15]

Shadd and Cuffe would not have agreed on *where* to relocate, though. Shadd was very much against the all-Black institutions that had become mainstays of the Black community in America. She didn't like segregation of any sort, regardless of what necessitated it. In fact, part of her resistance to Black preachers in America was the fact that they almost always pastored all-Black churches.

Where many Black abolitionists saw Black churches, communities, and businesses as safe havens from the white supremacy that beleaguered America, Mary Ann saw them as concessions to the segregation mindset Black Americans were supposed to be warring against. When she became the first Black woman publisher in North America (and the first woman publisher in Canada) by launching the *Provincial Freeman*, she spilled much ink castigating people and institutions in the abolitionist movement that history now hold in high esteem—people like Henry Highland Garnet, the object of Mary Ann Shadd's criticism at the beginning of this chapter.

Her eloquent boldness brought her many critics. One male journalist wrote: "Miss Shadd has said and written many things which we think will add nothing to her credit as a lady."[16]

Still, despite heated disagreement with more than one prominent abolitionist in her day, Shadd remained a vocal fixture of the movement, particularly in Canada. In 1858, she gave a speech in Chatham, Canada, that resonated throughout the coming years of the Civil War:

> The more readiness we Evince the more we manifest our love, and as our field is directly among those of his creatures made in his own image in acting as themselves who is no respecter of persons, we must have failed in our duty until we become decided to waive all prejudices of Education, birth, nation, or training and make the test of our obedience God's Equal command to love the neighbor as ourselves.[17]

In the spirit of her quest for *doing* when the Civil War broke out, Shadd departed Canada and returned to the United States to recruit for the Union Army. She was accompanied by many Black emigrants who saw the Civil War as an opportunity to fight for the freedom they had grown hopeless of ever seeing achieved in their homeland. Notably, Charlotte Forten's father, Robert, also came back from Canada to America to enlist and later die in the struggle for freedom.

How Should We Then Teach

Freedom did not put a halt to the disagreements that flew between Black activists. The *how* of freedom continued to divide educators for years to come.

Rather, the debate of the day concerned whether Black students would be better served by learning trades or liberal arts. Staunch commentators like Booker T. Washington maintained that the road to Black acceptance in white society was paved by respectability—and that that respectability could be best achieved by a trade. Racial uplift, he argued, would be the result of hard work and elbow grease.

On the opposite side of the spectrum, others maintained the importance of a liberal arts education, arguing that the way to gain traction in society was through the ability to participate in meaningful, intellectual discourse and to fight for equal rights regardless of respectability and trade.

Historian Jennifer Lund Smith writes:

> Black educators at the turn of the century engaged in a fierce debate about the merits of a liberal arts education versus a vocational education. Booker T. Washington, the founder of Tuskegee Institute, articulated the argument that African Americans needed vocational skills above all, to gain economic power and independence. W. E. B. Du Bois, who earned degrees at Fisk University and Harvard, and who taught economics and history at Atlanta University from 1897 to 1910, forcefully disagreed. He contended that intellectual parity would empower black Americans. In refusing to reject vocational education, Laney "mixed idealism and pragmatism." Furthermore, philanthropists tended to fund vocational schools, which they considered less threatening, more generously than liberal arts schools for black students, and the intense competition for benefactors' money most likely influenced Laney's decision to include vocational classes for her students.[18]

While W. E. B. Du Bois and Booker T. Washington are most often cited as the poster children of these two opposing views, many other teachers would fall along a wide spectrum from trade education to liberal arts. Some would even lose their jobs by focusing too much on liberal arts over more economically viable pursuits.

Unity in Diversity

The unity of Mary Ann Shadd, Henry Highland Garnett, and Frederick Douglass can be distilled into the theme of this book: Black Americans are made in the image of God and, as such, are invested with identity, dignity, and significance. *That* is the thread that holds them together. It is the same thread that runs through the work of Maria Stewart, Samuel Eli Cornish, Reverend Pennington, and Jarena Lee, despite their many disagreements. And it was through their diversity of thought that they held one another accountable and pushed the needle toward progress.

Paul Cuffe died in 1817 before seeing his dreams of emigration come to fruition. Historian Sally Loomis writes:

> Ironically, resistance to return to Africa helped spark the remarkable Black Abolitionist Movement that followed, for which Cuffe had helped pave the way by uniting blacks and furthering white abolitionist respect for blacks in America and England.[19]

Not only did Cuffe's words spur the abolitionist movement on America's shores, but they were also seeds that later bloomed in modern Pan-African thought.

As the civil rights movement of the 1950s and '60s morphed, activists embarked upon the age-old debate: Could America overcome its racist foundations to become a welcoming home for Black Americans? Was the work invested in that outcome worthy of the fruit produced so far? Or was Africa or another destination the place where Black Americans should go and start again?

Questions of women's rights and roles also came into play in this hundred-years-later version of the civil rights movement, as did echoes of respectability ideals and infighting. The book of Ecclesiastes famously proclaims there is nothing new under the sun, and when it comes to the diversity of opinion in *any* liberation movement, those verses ring incredibly true.

This chapter represents an important aside in the reclamation of the often obscured history of abolition in America. It is tempting to resort to hagiography[20]—caricatures and high-light reels—to venerate these long-forgotten names and under-reported strides, but doing so would be to engage in the same dishonest history this book intends to remedy.

When and how the enslaved should be freed, what should await them once freed, and what America should look like in the wake of that freedom differed from abolitionist to abolitionist—Black and white alike.

The one thing that unified the abolitionists profiled here is the undaunted belief in the humanity and inherent dignity of Black image bearers and their claim to the rights and privileges of American citizenship. There is more than enough to learn about that one kernel of truth without getting into the weeds of the other minutiae. But it's still important to point out that the "other minutiae" were extremely important and present in the lives of those that went before us.

There is nothing new under the sun.

And man should be allowed to walk free beneath that sun.

8

"God Gave Me That Freedom"

Nat Turner is an example of outright rebellion, but his was not the only way. Some of the enslaved rebelled by running away and claiming their freedom. Those claims to freedom eventually led to the Emancipation Proclamation and paved the way for future activism.

In April 1775, the loyalist governor of Virginia, James Murray, a fourth Earl of Dunmore, made a fateful proclamation. Fearing the mounting revolution in the thirteen colonies, he decided to enact martial law, promising that anyone who would bear arms on behalf of His Majesty's crown—indentured servants, Negroes, and others—would earn their freedom.

I do, in virtue of the power and authority to me given, *by his Majesty*, determine to execute martial law, and cause the same to be executed throughout this colony; and to the end that

151

peace and *good order* may the sooner be restored, I do require every person capable of bearing arms to resort to his Majesty's STANDARD, or be looked upon as traitors to his Majesty's crown and government, and thereby become liable to the penalty the law inflicts upon such offences, *such as forfeiture of life, confiscation of lands*, &c. &c. And I do hereby farther declare all *indented servants, Negroes*, or others (appertaining to rebels) *free*, that are able and willing to bear arms, they *joining his Majesty's troops*, as soon as may be, for the more speedily reducing this Colony to a *proper sense* of their duty, to his Majesty's crown and dignity.[1]

Virginia's slaveholders were terrified.

Not only did they fear losing their enslaved and indentured laborers, they also feared the repercussions of freed Blacks dwelling within their state borders.

The Virginians would not stand for it.

The *Pennsylvania Journal and Weekly Advisor* declared:

Here you have a Proclamation that will at once show the *baseness* of Lord Dunmore's heart, his *malice* and *treachery* against the people who were *once* under his government, and his *officious* violation of all law, justice and humanity; not to mention his *arrogating* to himself a power which neither he can assume, nor any power upon earth invest him with.[2]

Lord Dunmore's "malice" and "treachery" were met with swift reprisal by the Virginia Committee of Safety. They released a statement entitled "Caution to Negroes":

The second class of people for whose sake a few remarks upon this proclamation seem necessary is the Negroes. They have been flattered with their freedom if they be able to bear arms and will speedily join Lord Dunmore's troops. To none of them is freedom promised but to such as are able to do Lord Dunmore's service. The aged, the infirm, the women, the children are still to remain the property of their masters, who will be provoked to severity should part of their slaves desert them. Lord Dunmore's declaration, then, is a cruel declaration to the Negroes. He does not pretend to make it out of any tenderness to them, but solely on his own account, and should it meet with success it leaves by far the greater number at the mercy of an enraged and injured people. But should there be any among the Negroes weak enough to believe that Lord Dunmore intends to do them a kindness and wicked enough to provoke the fury of the Americans against their defenseless fathers and mothers, their wives, their women, and their children, let them only consider the difficulty of effecting their escape and what they must expect to suffer if they fall into the hands of the Americans.[3]

Enslaved families were routinely separated—husbands barred from protecting their wives, mothers stripped of their children. In the coming years, this trend would become a defining characteristic of chattel slavery. And yet, Virginia leveled a threat against anyone tempted to accept Dunmore's offer: "You can't take everyone with you, and it would be a shame if some angry planters exacted revenge on your elderly, your wives, and your daughters."

This threat was not even thinly veiled—it was an outright fearmongering tactic to keep Black men from joining the ranks of the British.

And it failed.

Over one hundred thousand enslaved men and women answered the call. Some of the men became part of Dunmore's Ethiopian regiment while the women worked for the British soldiers in any way they could be useful. Others sought refuge in British camps, clinging to a tenuous promise of freedom from one slaveholding country in the bosom of another.

When the fog of war ended, most of these souls did not achieve the freedom they envisioned. Some were sold back to their masters, others escaped to British colonies, and still others eked out a living in the newly founded Americas. But chattel slavery raged on in the country founded on equality and fraternity. In *Running from Bondage*, historian Karen Cook Bell notes,

While the vast majority remained enslaved in a new nation whose 1787 Constitution endorsed the slave system by providing for the return of runaway slaves, the quest for freedom through flight remained one of the most enduring occurrences throughout the era of slavery.[4]

Who Makes Men Free

Amy Post, a Quaker abolitionist, wrote a postscript to her friend Harriet Jacobs's autobiography, *Incidents in the Life of a Slave Girl*, the fantastical and completely true tale of Linda Brent (Harriet's pseudonym). In it, Amy documented Linda's indignation at having her freedom bought for her some years after she had escaped to the North of her own accord.

This Empire State is a shabby place of refuge for the oppressed; but here, through anxiety, turmoil, and despair, the freedom of Linda and her children was finally secured, by the exertions of a generous friend. She was grateful for the boon; **but the idea of having been bought was always galling to a spirit that could never acknowledge itself to be a chattel.** She wrote to us thus, soon after the event: **"I thank you for your kind expressions in**

regard to my freedom; but the freedom I had before the money
was paid was dearer to me. God gave me that freedom; but
man put God's image in the scales with the paltry sum of three
hundred dollars. I served for my liberty as faithfully as Jacob
served for Rachel. At the end, he had large possessions; but I
was robbed of my victory; I was obliged to resign my crown,
to rid myself of a tyrant."[5]

Harriet Jacobs chose freedom for herself before it was ever
purchased by benevolent white folks. But more than that, she
was *born* free because she had been made in God's image.
Three hundred dollars was a "paltry sum" for a being with a
soul, and it tried Harriet's spirit that she had to submit to the
dollars and cents of slavery to have a moment's peace once
the Fugitive Slave Act of 1850 was passed. She saw the piece
of paper releasing her as property of Dr. James Norcum as a
relinquishment of the victory she took for herself the minute
she decided to escape.

And Harriet was not alone in these feelings.

Self-emancipation had been a theme among the enslaved
since their first arrival on America's shores. Whether "lying
out" (running away for short periods of time with the intent
of eventually coming back)[6] or making a calculated break for
the North, the enslaved resisted their enslavement. They did
so not by virtue of reading abolitionist literature nor through
knowledge of a world in which they could be equal to their
enslavers. They sought freedom because they knew—inherently,
as all men know—they were born to be free.

Stories of escape and resistance have traditionally centered
on men, but a growing number of historians are setting the
record straight. Karen Cook Bell, Carol Berkin, Stephanie
M. H. Camp, and others have shared testimonies of enslaved
women who ran, resisted, and rebelled right alongside their
male counterparts.

After the Civil War, the South would look back on slavery with more than a hint of nostalgia. It shaped the Southern imagination, picturing the happy slave who loved the master's children more than her own, who would do anything to preserve the life of their dear masters, who saw rebellion as an unthinkable anomaly.

But when the opportunity arose, the enslaved asserted their independence.

And the Civil War provided the perfect opportunity for escape.

The Mounting Conflict

Southerners were beginning to see the writing on the wall. As America moved westward, more and more territories decided against welcoming the enslaved into their borders. These motions were happening for several reasons:

- **To create equal opportunity for all white settlers.** Some thought it would be impossible for the common man to keep up with slave owners' access to free labor in the new land.
- **To avoid the barbarism of slavery.** Even if many white Americans did not consider Black Americans equal, they did find slavery an unsavory institution.
- **To avoid the proliferation of Black people in the American West.** Like Missouri, other new states considered barring free Black people *and* slaves from their territory, essentially outlawing Black people altogether.

It's important to note that abolition is nowhere on this list. Still, Southerners saw the legislation as an affront to their participation in westward expansion. How were they to take part in Manifest Destiny without the enslaved to till the soil and harvest their crops?

Congressman David Wilmot moved to ban slavery in all the territories acquired in the Mexican–American War because

> I make no war upon the South nor upon slavery in the South. I have no squeamish sensitiveness upon the subject of slavery, nor morbid sympathy for the slave. I plead the cause of the rights of white freemen. I would preserve for free white labor a fair country, a rich inheritance, where the sons of toil, of my own race and own color, can live without the disgrace which association with negro slavery brings upon free labor.[7]

Many Americans—both slaveholding and non—agreed with him.

In 1857, Dredd Scott sued for his freedom on the grounds that much of his servitude had been carried out in free states where it was illegal to hold slaves. In the long and grueling proceedings that followed, Scott won his freedom suit on the state level only to eventually lose it on the national stage. Throughout American history, there are examples of Black Americans laying claim to the rights of the citizenship that they believed the founding documents promised to all of America's residents. Yet, by the time Scott's case arrived at the Supreme Court, those rights were as hotly contested as they had ever been.

Supreme Court Justice Roger B. Taney wrote in his decision:

> In the opinion of the court, the legislation and histories of the times, and the language used in the Declaration of Independence, show, that neither the class of persons who had been imported as slaves, nor their descendants, whether they had become free or not, were then acknowledged as a part of the people [citizens of the United States].[8]

The Civil War started because the South saw a threat to the expansion of slavery. Not because the highest courts in the land were trending toward equality for Black people. This distinction becomes all the more important when homing in on the self-emancipation of the enslaved.

After Abraham Lincoln's election, Southerners felt their "right" to own slaves was hanging in the balance. South Carolina became the first state to secede, declaring:

> The General Government, as the common agent, passed laws to carry into effect these stipulations of the States. For many years these laws were executed. **But an increasing hostility on the part of the non-slaveholding States to the institution of slavery, has led to a disregard of their obligations,** and the laws of the General Government have ceased to effect the objects of the Constitution.[9]

Mississippi put it this way:

> Our position is **thoroughly identified with the institution of slavery**—the greatest material interest of the world. Its labor supplies the product which constitutes by far the largest and most important portions of commerce of the earth. These products are peculiar to the climate verging on the tropical regions, and by an imperious law of nature, none but the black race can bear exposure to the tropical sun. These products have become necessities of the world, **and a blow at slavery is a blow at commerce and civilization.** That blow has been long aimed at the institution, and was at the point of reaching its consummation. There was no choice left us but submission to the mandates of abolition, or a dissolution of the Union, whose principles had been subverted to work out our ruin.[10]

Texas had this to say:

> She [Texas] was received as a commonwealth holding, **maintaining and protecting the institution known as negro slavery—the servitude of the African to the white race within her limits**—a

relation that had existed from the first settlement of her wilderness by the white race, and which her people intended should exist in all future time.[11]

The Southern states were so aligned with slavery—and the white supremacy that precipitated it—they cited their inalienable rights as citizens when moving to protect it in 1860. As the pieces fell into place for the Civil War, the Southern cause became even clearer through a speech given by the vice president of the Confederacy, Alexander Stephens:

> Our new government is founded upon exactly the opposite idea; **its foundations are laid, its corner-stone rests, upon the great truth that the negro is not equal to the white man;** that slavery subordination to the superior race is his natural and normal condition. This, our new government, is the first, in the history of the world, based upon this great physical, philosophical, and moral truth.[12]

The notion that Black Americans were even *American* was ridiculous to Southern slaveholders, and the idea of equality insulted them in the extreme. In 1837, years before secession, Senator (and two-time Vice President) John C. Calhoun stated:

> We of the South will not, cannot, surrender our institutions. To maintain the existing relations between the two races inhabiting that section of the Union, it is indispensable to the peace and happiness of both. It **cannot be subverted without drenching the country in blood**, and extirpating one or the other of the races. Be it good or bad, it has grown up with our society and institutions, and is so interwoven with them that to destroy it would be to destroy us as a people.[13]

It is important to let the white supremacists of the South speak for themselves because shortly after the Civil War, they began rewriting their reasoning for entering the bloodiest conflict America would ever see.

Abraham Lincoln famously stated that if he could preserve the Union without freeing a single slave, he would.[14] These are not the words of someone who loved slavery, but those of a leader being torn apart by the issue. For the North, the Civil War was about preserving the Union. Some abolitionists fought and died to end slavery, but most Northern soldiers fought and died to preserve the nation.

It was the Southern soldiers who fought to preserve slavery—and not just slaveholders, who were wealthy enough not to have to go to war themselves. Slavery wasn't just about the actual personal ownership of Black property—it was about white supremacy. White Southerners saw the enslaved as belonging to a different class of people, and the idea that they could one day be free was a nightmarish proposition.

In the popular Southern newspaper *De Bow's Review*, De Bow himself pointed out that slavery wasn't just about individual ownership. It was aspirational. It was proper. It was a way of life.

Whose Idea Was Freedom?

Slave rebellion usually resulted in a crackdown on Black literacy. Slaveholders reasoned that if their property could not read abolitionist texts, they could not absorb abolitionist ideals.

What they failed to recognize was that abolitionist ideals did not come from the writings and speeches of abolitionists, but from within. As Jacobs said, "God gave me that freedom." Her autonomy was inherent, something vested in her the moment she was created as a human being made in the image of God.

And American slaveholders understood this for themselves. Consider again a slaveholder's words in the Declaration of Independence: "We hold these truths to be self-evident, that all men are created equal, that they are endowed by their Creator with certain unalienable Rights, that among these are Life, Liberty and the pursuit of Happiness."

Consider the words of the man who inspired Jefferson, John Locke: "Men being, as has been said, by nature, all free, equal and independent, no one can be put out of this estate, and subjected to the political power of another, without his own consent."[15]

Slaveholders belonged to a rich legacy of self-liberation from an overreach of power. It was a liberation fueled by Enlightenment text and their understanding of the Bible, but if their ideology about man being *born* free and equal was correct, then that knowledge had to come from within.

Except, of course, if it should somehow come from within the body and mind of the enslaved. In their quest to vilify abolitionists, slaveholders were shocked to find that, given the opportunity to flee, the enslaved chose to go willingly. Not only that, but they chose to risk life and limb to aid those who might free them.

"During the war," according to historian William Barney, "Southern whites were shocked to discover that the average domestic slave would be far more likely to lead Union soldiers to the family silver rather than to hide and guard it."[16]

After the Civil War started, an influx of enslaved refugees poured into Union camps.

In 1850, the Fugitive Slave Act became the latest in a string of compromises the federal government made to appease the South's desire to keep slavery alive and well in the Union. As previously discussed, this law not only made it illegal for any Northerner to aid and abet runaway enslaved people; it also compelled Northerners who knew about fugitive slaves to work with slaveholders for their return. We've already seen how Frances Ellen Watkins Harper and others responded to the implications of this legislation.

After the Civil War began, the Fugitive Slave Act presented a conundrum for Union troops. Enslaved people who lived near enough to Union camps were breaking free and approaching them for sanctuary. Under the Fugitive Slave Act, the Union soldiers were breaking federal law by allowing the formerly enslaved to stay. However, as the South was in rebellion, they did not want to facilitate returning the Southern labor force. And so the seeds of contraband camps were born.

At the start of the war, the Union had no policy to deal with the African Americans seeking protection. Individual commanders made their own decisions. Some commanders put them to work for Union troops while others returned them to plantation owners. At Fort Monroe in Hampton, Virginia, Union Maj. General Benjamin Butler refused to send three fugitives back into the bonds of slavery. He classified the escaping slaves as contraband of war. This term meant that once the fleeing slaves crossed Union army lines, they were classified as property. All enemy property that fell into Union hands constituted contraband and would not be returned. Because of Butler's actions, a federal policy was instituted on August 6, 1861—fugitive slaves were declared to be 'contraband of war' if their labor had been used to aid the Confederacy in any way. If found to be contraband, they were declared free.[17]

General Butler was not an abolitionist, and had, in fact, voted for Jefferson Davis in the past. However, he knew that withholding the runaways was a smart tactical move. It removed responsibility from the Union soldiers to abide by the Fugitive Slave Act because the Southern states' rebellion made that act null and void. Further, it played on the Southern laws that dehumanized enslaved people by treating them as property: now, that "property" was considered the spoils of war.

Contraband camps began to crop up all over the Union-occupied South, particularly in Georgia and South Carolina.

This living contraband represented the innate desire of the enslaved to pursue freedom on their own terms. It was *their* movement that prodded the Union to take steps toward legislating their freedom. *Their* innate quest for equality forced the Union's hand. Many credit this massive migration of the enslaved as the impetus for the Emancipation Proclamation.

Abraham Lincoln, called the Great Emancipator, saw several factors in the reality of contraband camps: enslaved people who had left their enslavers could no longer aid in the Southern war effort; enslaved men represented valuable manpower for the Union Army; and an executive order would stir even more of the enslaved to take their freedom into their own hands. The proclamation followed the moves the enslaved were already making on their own behalf. In the words of W. E. B. Du Bois: "With perplexed and laggard steps, the United States Government followed the footsteps of the black slave" toward freedom.[18]

Often, the stories told cast the enslaved as helpless pawns tossed to and fro by the whims of the powers that be. Even as modern readers understand that the enslaved were not *actually*

Photographer James F. Gibson

Contraband camp

property but people, this narrative treats them as such. If they needed white abolitionists to free them—if they needed the Emancipation Proclamation to give them the idea to run—if they needed to be told that they were ill-used by the Slave Power of the South, then they did not have the innate rights of which Locke and Jefferson so eloquently wrote. If they needed to be rescued instead of being intent on rescuing themselves, this story is about the heroism of white saviors.

Du Bois offers a helpful reframe: the government *followed the footsteps* of the slave. This was not just about slavery, but about *personhood*. These people, created in the image of God, had the same inalienable rights as their white neighbors, and like their white neighbors, they were willing to fight for them.

And had been fighting for a long time.

Bury Me in the Ocean

The math of a slave ship was often complex.

There would be a handful of crew members, and anywhere from two hundred and fifty to six hundred newly enslaved Africans. The male captives were usually kept under the deck, chained together in closer-than-close quarters to stave off potential uprisings. Some captains of slave ships overpacked their cargo, surmising they could make up for the inevitable deaths at sea by packing in more bodies. Others kept the cargo holds less crowded in hopes of staving off the disease that so often beleaguered transatlantic travel.

In either case, African women were usually kept above deck for the entertainment of the slave catchers. Captain James Barbot recorded in 1770:

> Toward the evening the women slaves diverted themselves on the deck, as they thought fit, some conversing together, others

dancing, singing, and sporting after their manner, which pleased them highly, and often made us pastime . . . many of them sprightly maidens full of jollity and good humor, afforded us abundance of recreations; as did several little fine boys, which we mostly kept to attend us about the ship.[19]

Because enslaved women were often above deck for easy access to the whims of the ship's crew, they were also the first to rebel. Historian Rebecca Hall found that the more women on a slave ship, the more likely a rebellion was to take place. Whether fashioning weapons, fighting tooth and nail with bare hands, or plunging themselves into the ocean to die to avoid being taken

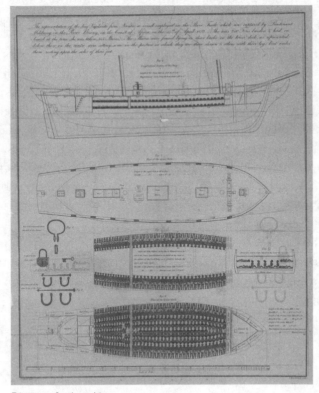

Diagram of a slave ship

across the sea, the enslaved fought for their freedom from the very beginning.

Because that freedom, that liberty, that dignity is innate.

The fighting did not stop once the enslaved made their way over the Atlantic. The history of slave rebellions has been obscured—by Southern historians who wanted to portray the enslaved as happy serfs to their masters, by Northern abolitionists who saw themselves as the heroes of the enslaved, by a country's history that only recognizes some of its patriots. But men and women *did* rebel throughout the history of enslavement in America.

The civil rights movement did not crop up in the 1940s, '50s, and '60s unbidden by historical precedent. Before Black students sat at lunch counters, occupied buses, or tried to enroll in colleges, the actions of enslaved men and women catalyzed an activist network birthed at America's inception.

In the case of the Stono Rebellion in 1739, it had been taking shape even before the country became the United States of America. Whether it was young people risking detainment at Mississippi's infamous Parchman Prison in the 1960s, Harriet Jacobs stowing away in a dank crawl space in the 1840s, or a group of newly enslaved Africans rising up to fight against their captors in the 1720s, the enslaved have always fought back. Because as human beings made in God's image, they had an innate sense of their worth given by God.

The Civil War was waged for a litany of reasons, but the enslaved made sure their freedom became a central conflict of the struggle. Through their own valiant self-emancipation, they changed the course of the war.

They changed the course of history.

9

"As Scarce as Hen's Teeth"

The religious fervor and fidelity of the enslaved developed in spite of their legislated illiteracy and lack of access to the Bible. They developed a robust religious fidelity in spite of the fact that they often weren't allowed to hold their own religious meetings, and had much to say about the nature of their enslavers' religion. Their Christianity often fueled their life and practice after freedom.[1]

Thomas Lewis Johnson was eighteen years old when Anthony Burns was recaptured.

There was a slave on our lot named Anthony Burnes, who managed to get to Boston. Under the fugitive slave law he was brought back to Richmond, Virginia, and put into the slave pen for sale. Young Mr. Brent came to me one day when Burnes was in the trader's pen, and told me that Anthony was in gaol. He knew how to write, and had written himself a pass and had gone to the north, and that his master and other gentlemen had brought him back, and now he would be sold to Georgia. All this, said he, Burnes brought upon himself because he knew how to write. "Lor's o'er me," I said, "is dat so?" He answered very gravely, "Yes, that is so."[2]

Little did Mr. Brent know that Thomas himself had been learning to read and write for as long as he could remember. Like Black mothers would do for years to come, Thomas's mother taught him that literacy was the key to his freedom—and like Black children would do for generations after, Thomas cherished his mother's wisdom in his heart.

The road to literacy was not an easy one for an enslaved young man. Thomas was born in 1836, five short years after Nat Turner's rebellion shocked the South, leading to tightened restrictions on teaching the enslaved. According to author Janet Duitsman Cornelius:

> Georgia in 1829 provided fines, whipping, or imprisonment for anyone teaching slaves or free blacks to read or write. In 1830 a provision of the Louisiana slave code stated "that all persons who shall teach, or permit or cause to be taught, any slave in this State to read or write, shall be imprisoned not less than one or more than twelve months." North Carolina also forbade teaching or giving books to slaves in an 1830 law, since such teaching "has a tendency to excite dissatisfaction in their minds and produce insurrection . . ." In its 1830–31 legislative session, Virginia provided penalties for whites who assembled with Negroes to teach reading or writing, or who taught any slave for pay. After Nat Turner, Virginians also prohibited teaching by slaves or free Negroes. Alabama also prohibited, under fine, the attempt to teach any slave or free person of color to spell, read, or write. South Carolina's law restricting black literacy, though not passed until several years after the others in 1834, was the most sweeping.[3]

Southern slaveholders saw literacy as a decisive step toward slave rebellions, pointing to the words of David Walker and the actions of Nat Turner as proof they needed to quell it.

As a South Carolinian put it, there could be no mass literacy in the South "until man can eat of the tree of knowledge and not know evil." He insisted that bans on black literacy would have to continue "until those of our negroes who are taught to read the Bible, shall be unable to read Walker's pamphlet."[4]

Thomas, who was Virginia born and bred, lived in the heart of the most strident educational restrictions for the enslaved. But he was undaunted. Not only did he want to be free, he wanted to be a minister. And as such, he understood the importance of learning to read the Bible.

> Soon after my conversion I felt a deep desire to preach the Gospel. But two difficulties presented themselves: first, I was a slave, for though I had a free soul, yet my body was in slavery; then, second, I could not read the Bible with much understanding, and there was no way for me to succeed but the old way, that was, by taking advantage of every opportunity to learn all I could.[5]

These educational opportunities most often presented themselves through his much younger master. Thomas was skilled in the art of finessing his enslavers to achieve the knowledge he desired. This art was a matter of survival, yes, but also of rebellion and resistance.

Peter Randolph tells the story of an enslaved man who employed this skill to mock his master to his face when the master asked his slave how he looked:

> "Oh massa, mighty!" "What do you mean mighty, Pompey?" "Why massa, you look noble." "What do you mean by noble?" "Why, sar, you look just like one lion." "Why, Pompey, where have you seen a lion?" "I seen one down in yonder field the other day, massa." "Pompey, you foolish fellow, that was a *jackass*!" "Was it, massa? Well, you look just like him."[6]

Thomas's version of this posturing took place when his young master was working with his spelling books.

> At night, when the young master would be getting his lessons, I used to choose some word I wanted to know how to spell, and say, "Master, I'll bet you can't spell 'looking-glass.'" He would at once spell it. I would exclaim, "Lor's o'er me, you can spell nice." Then I would go out and spell the word over and over again. I knew that once it was in my head it would never be got out again. This young man was very kind, and was always willing to answer my questions. But sometimes he would ask why I wanted to know, and I would say, "I want to see how far you are." In the course of time he would often read portions of his lessons to me. If I liked this and wanted to hear it again, I would say, "Lor's o'er me, read that again," which he often did. In this way each week I added a little to my small store of knowledge about the great world in which I lived.[7]

Once Thomas was able to get his hands on a spelling book of his own, he had all the ingredients he needed to continue his self-education—and continue, he did.

Reading the Word

One of the consistent charges brought against white Southerners aimed at the fact that their bans on reading kept the enslaved from reading the Bible for themselves. America was a largely Protestant nation, one founded on principles of religious fundamentalism and independence, and yet, an entire class of people was kept from reading and understanding the Bible for themselves. Instead, they were forced to rely on white preachers to distill the Word of God for them.

One abolitionist stated:

> Some of you can read, such know the advantages of it; you who cannot, strive to acquire that knowledge. Surely this knowledge

is an object of great importance, were it only for the opportunity it affords of becoming acquainted with the best of books, the Bible. The holy Scriptures of the old and new testament, contain invaluable treasures of instruction, and of comfort. It would give us much satisfaction, could we oftener see them in the hands of those who are able to read them, and that an increasing anxiety to become possessed of their contents, and to profit by their precepts, might be more observed among you.[8]

But the Word of God was a critical type of literature enslavers sought to keep out of the hands of the enslaved, lest they get the "wrong idea" about what they were due from their enslavers.

Indeed, when Thomas Johnson was first converted, he had a hard time finding a church where he felt at home. "In Richmond there were Churches of coloured people, but they had white Pastors, who never failed to keep us informed about Abraham's servants, and as to the injunction to Hagar."[9] Josiah Henson talked about how, in Maryland, he first heard a part of the Bible preached that he'd never heard in any of the religious services he attended as an enslaved man:

> When I arrived at the place of meeting, the services were so far advanced that the speaker was just beginning his discourse from the text Hebrews 11:9, "that he, by the grace of God, should taste death for every man." This was the first text of the Bible to which I had ever listened, knowing it to be such. I have never forgotten it, and scarce a day has passed since in which I have not recalled it, and the sermon that was preached from it.[10]

In the British West Indies, fear of the enslaved using passages from the Bible to encourage rebellion was so severe that a slave Bible was produced. It cut out about 90 percent of the Old Testament and 50 percent of the New Testament, paying close attention to Exodus and any other passage that hinted at the inherent dignity of all men.

The book of Psalms was missing entirely. What might it have been like for an enslaved man or woman to read the words of Psalm 8:5–8?

> For thou hast made him a little lower than the angels, and hast **crowned him with glory and honour.**
> Thou madest him to have dominion over the works of thy hands; thou hast put all things under his feet:
> All sheep and oxen, yea, and the beasts of the field;
> The fowl of the air, and the fish of the sea, and whatsoever passeth through the paths of the seas.

So many enslaved men and women in America would die having never known them.

A Biblical Education

Nevertheless, modern readers should not make the mistake of believing this lack of access to the Bible meant the enslaved failed to receive a Christian education or that they saw Christianity as the white man's religion. They forged a religious education with their own hands, apart from what they were taught (or not taught) by their enslavers.

Thomas L. Webber's 1973 book, *Deep Like the Rivers: Education in the Slave Quarter Community, 1831–1865*, contains a chapter titled "True Christianity versus Slaveholding Priestcraft: The Immorality of Slavery." In it, he outlines the way the enslaved often perceived the so-called Christianity of their enslavers as something completely different from the true Christianity they practiced.

Another formerly enslaved man, John Brown, said, "I have often been asked how we slaves, being so ignorant, come to know that holding a human creature as a slave is wrong and wicked." He replied:

I say that, putting the cruelties of the system out of the question, we cannot be made to understand how any man can hold another man as a slave, and do right. A slave is not a human being in the eye of the law, and the slaveholder looks upon him just as what the law makes him; nothing more, and perhaps even something less. **But God made every man to stand upright before him, and if the slave law throws that man down . . . then the law unmakes God's work**; the slaveholder lends himself to it, and not all the reasoning or arguments that can be strung together, on a text or on none, can make the thing right. I have long heard preachments from the ministers of the Gospel to try and show that slavery is not a wrong system; but somehow they could not fix it right in my mind, and they always seemed to me to have a hard matter to bring it square to their own.[11]

William Craft credited the treatment of enslavers toward the enslaved as giving him a "thorough hatred, not for true Christianity, but for slaveholding piety."[12]

WILLIAM CRAFT.

ELLEN CRAFT.

National Portrait Gallery, Smithsonian Institution

Frances Ellen Watkins Harper, though never enslaved, encapsulated the thoughts of many an enslaved person toward Christianity in her book *Iola Leroy* when she recorded the conversation of two enslaved men describing the type of Christianity practiced by their enslavers:

Oh, I don't take much stock in white folks' religion, said Robert, laughing carelessly. The way, said Tom Anderson, dat some of dese folks cut their cards yere, I think dey'll be as sceece in hebben as hen's teeth. I

173

think wen some of dem preachers brings de Bible 'round an' tells us 'bout mindin' our marsters and not stealin' dere tings, dat dey preach to please de white folks, an' dey frows coleness ober de meetin'.[13]

Despite the religious persecution endured by the enslaved— for what else would you call not being allowed to read the Bible, gather to pray, or practice biblically and legally binding marriage—they maintained a thorough understanding of the gospel. Rather than being turned away from the practice of Christianity by their oppression, many enslaved people saw the Christianity practiced by their enslavers as a counterfeit gospel.

In fact, many of the "quarter community," as Webber refers to the enslaved, determined the only way for a slaveholder to show true conversion was to free all the people he had enslaved. Like the rich young ruler, they surmised the true sign of following Jesus as giving up the worldly treasure of Black bodies in pursuit of true righteousness.

This conviction was not reserved for cruel masters alone. Many enslaved men and women taught that *all* white Americans who practiced chattel slavery were consigned to hell. "For quarter blacks the very act of holding slaves was sufficient to cause even the most benevolent master's soul to be damned."[14]

Aaron Siddles declared, "By the law of Almighty God, I was born free, by the law of man a slave." He stated further:

We believe slavery to be a sin—always, everywhere, and only sin. Sin itself, apart from the occasional rigors incidental to its administration, and from all those perils, liabilities, and positive inflictions to which its victims are continually exposed. Sin is in the nature of the act which created it, and in the elements which constitute it. **Sin, because it converts persons into things; men into property; God's image into merchandise.** Because it forbids men from using themselves for the advancement of their own well-being, and turns them into mere instruments to be used by others solely for the benefit of the users. **Because it constitutes one man the owner of the body and spirit of other men; gives him power and permission to make his pecuniary profit the very end of their being, thus striking them out of existence as beings, possessing rights and susceptibilities of happiness, and forcing them to exist merely as appendages of his own existence, in other words, because slavery holds and uses men as mere means for which to accomplish ends, of which end, their own interests are not to be part.** Thus annihilating the sacred and eternal distinction between a person and a thing; a distinction proclaimed an axiom of all human consciousness; a distinction created by God.[15]

It is important to look for the testimony of the enslaved wherever it can be found. It is the only way to bypass the skewed historical narrative that laymen have so often imbibed. Despite the roadblocks to literacy, the enslaved passed on their testimonies in myriad ways.

Wade in the Water

The legislation against enslaved literacy is a well-known fact, and yet too often the far-reaching implications escape our notice—particularly in a Christian context. In a time where people were starting to take advantage of the opportunity to read the Bible and pass on its knowledge, the enslaved were barred from the privilege of reading the Word for themselves.

But that does not mean that the enslaved didn't find ways to pass on the truths of the Christian religion to one another—even when that religion didn't gel with the behavior of their enslavers.

When Charlotte Forten Grimké became a missionary teacher in the Port Royal Experiment, she wrote two articles in *The Atlantic* outlining her experience among the formerly enslaved.

In them, she shared the Negro spirituals she so often heard sung by her pupils. She wasn't the only one to notice the trend of singing among the enslaved. Many viewed the act as evidence that they were living merrily in bondage.

Nothing could be further from the truth. Often, that singing was a sign of outright rebellion akin to the literacy from which the enslaved were barred.

> And de moon will turn to blood,
> And de moon will turn to blood,
> And de moon will turn to blood,
> In dat day—O-yoy, my soul!
> And de moon will turn to blood in that day.
> And you'll see de stars a'fallin
> And de world will be on fire,
> And you'll hear de saints a-singin'
> And de Lord will say to de sheep
> For to go to Him right hand
> But de goats must go to de left[16]

Webber records this song after sharing the following story:

> Slaves also deceive whites through the artful use of words and gesture. Often they were able to communicate seditious thoughts to each other under their master's very nose. A white man, the Reverend J.G. Williams, recorded the sermon of a Gullah preacher by the name of Brudder Coteny. In one of these sermons he ends with reference to the biblical declaration that God will separate the sheep from the goats on Judgement day. "What the Reverend Mr. Williams apparently missed," according to Genovese, "was that black folklore assigns a special meaning to goats: they are white people. He ought not have missed the special meaning assigned by ante-bellum whites to sheep: they were akin to blacks since both had 'wool,' not hair. The slaves did not miss the reference, for they roared back at Brudder Coteny, 'Bless de Lawd, we nigger know who hab de wool!'"[17]

176

Now read the lyrics to that spiritual again:

> And de Lord will say to de sheep
> For to go to Him right hand
> But de goats must go to de left[18]

Additionally, the enslaved used music to communicate when they were going on a trip. For a short journey, they might use the following song:

> Master and mistress both gone away,
> Gone down to Charleston to spend the summer day.
> I'm off to Charleston early in the mornin'
> To spend another day.[19]

For a longer bout, such as an escape attempt, they might turn to another song. *Follow the Drinking Gourd* heralded literal directions to freedom: wait for winter to end, follow the bank of the river and the marks on the trees, go north until you meet the Ohio River.

> When the sun comes back
> And the first quail calls
> Follow the Drinking Gourd,
> For the old man is waiting for to carry you to freedom,
> If you follow the Drinking Gourd
> The river bank makes a mighty good road,
> The dead trees show you the way.
> Left foot, peg foot, traveling on,
> Follow the Drinking Gourd
> The river ends between two hills,
> Follow the Drinking Gourd
> There's another river on the other side,
> Follow the Drinking Gourd
> When the great big river meets the little river,
> Follow the Drinking Gourd

When the great big river meets the little river,
Follow the Drinking Gourd.
For the old man is a-waiting to carry you to freedom,
If you follow the Drinking Gourd.

This was no happy-go-lucky whistling while they worked. These were hope-filled lyrics pointing to the promise of freedom. They were also the storytelling language of a people who had been kept illiterate by force. The enslaved could not pass their wisdom through the written word, so songs became a tool for education and communication.

And even when the songs were "just" spirituals longing for eternal rest across the Jordan, the enslaved held a hope beyond what the enslaver could see. They saw themselves as serving a completely different God than those who owned them.

Calling Out Hypocrisy

When the Civil War ended, the formerly enslaved flocked to schools in droves, both the young and the old. Maria Fearing was in her thirties when emancipation came, and she sat in a schoolroom with children less than a third her age, humbling herself before her teachers to learn to read the Bible for herself. Black women like Charlotte Forten Grimké, Sara G. Stanley, Mary S. Peake, and others answered the call to teach the formerly enslaved where they had once been barred from doing so. According to scholar Heather A. Williams:

> As they attempted to take control of their own lives, many freed-people wanted one thing more than all others: to learn to read and write. In slavery, the very act of learning to read had been a secret form of resistance, but in its aftermath, freedpeople transformed the act of becoming literate from a clandestine occurrence into one of life's necessities. Secret readings of newspapers had kept enslaved people informed of political debates

178

whose outcomes could determine their fates. Writing a pass had allowed slaves to move about without owners' knowledge. Literacy held the promise of entry into the public discourse concerning the destiny of African Americans in the United States.[20]

However, it would be a mistake to see this newfound access to education as a *new* formulation of thoughts and convictions. The enslaved had had an education *before* they became freed people because they were *people* even in bondage: intelligent beings created in God's image who forged a culture and values they passed on to their children. Part of that culture was calling out the hypocrisy of their enslavers.

With freedom, they found themselves in an even better position to do so.

Ida B. Wells was born in Mississippi in 1862. She was a daughter of two enslaved parents who understood the key that education represented for her future. After a brief stint as a teacher, she aimed her literacy at the press, reporting broadly about the white supremacy of the South and one of its most gruesome tools: lynching.

Long past the days of the slave quarters, calling out the hypocrisy of the American church became a mainstay of the civil rights movement. In the early twentieth century, while traveling through London, delivering speeches about America's legacy of lynching, Ida quipped:

MISS GARRITY.
PHOTOGRAPHER.   CHICAGO

Ida B. Wells-Barnett

National Portrait Gallery, Smithsonian Institution

Again the question was asked where were all the legal and civil authorities of the country, to say nothing of the Christian churches, that they permitted such things to be? I could only

179

say that despite the axiom that there is a remedy for every wrong, everybody in authority from the President of the United States down, had declared their inability to do anything; and that the Christian bodies and moral associations do not touch the question. It is the easiest way to get along in the South (and those portions in the North where lynchings take place) to ignore the question altogether; **our American Christians are too busy saving the souls of white Christians from burning in hell-fire to save the lives of black ones from present burning in fires kindled by white Christians.** The feelings of the people who commit these acts must not be hurt by protesting against this sort of thing, and so the bodies of the victims of mob hate must be sacrificed, and the country disgraced because of that fear to speak out.[21]

She understood the religion that so often masqueraded as Christianity in the South. She saw through the façade of slave-holders who boldly sat in church on Sunday after terrorizing the enslaved during the week—whipping husbands, sexually assaulting wives, selling off children, and taking part in what Frances Ellen Watkins Harper called the "fearful alchemy by which this blood can be transformed into gold."[22] She recognized how virtuous womanhood was lauded when it applied to the fragility and protected status of white womanhood; but she also knew how Black women were scorned in efforts of cultural femininity. She witnessed how white children were worthy of being nurtured and taught in the admonition of the Lord while Black children were considered unfit for literacy and learning because they were beasts of burden.

She watched when emancipation changed slave status according to the law but not according to the hearts of the white supremacists of the South. The belief remained that Black Americans were not truly made in the image of God or vested with dignity and significance that should keep them from the brutality that Southerners continued committing against them.

Ida B. Wells knew what so many Black sons and daughters of the South had *always* known, but she was uniquely blessed with the tools to communicate it. She said what so many Black sons and daughters of the South had been saying for hundreds of years but with the means to deliver the message far and wide. Literacy and access were important tools for disseminating the truths the enslaved already *knew* in their bones.

Thomas Lewis Johnson's mother told him that education was the key to his freedom, just like James Forten's father taught him that ships were the key to his independence. They taught these lessons not from a place of thorough, classical education nor from a place of recognized rights and privileges as American citizens. They themselves were not afforded the privileges they hoped their children would be afforded or those future generations would fight for. Nonetheless, they understood the fact that they were *worthy* of such privileges, and that inherent worth was impetus enough to fight.

They fought in pulpits, in newspaper print, and on the front lines of the Civil War. They fought in classrooms, in slave quarters, and on the Underground Railroad. They fought with pen, and sword, word and deed. They fought for the generation they could see and the future generations they could not. And whether they left a testament behind for us to read, they left a testimony through their survival, as well as their children's children, like the daughter writing these words.

These men and women—these image bearers—were born free. And no matter how they fought to achieve the physical manifestation of their spiritual freedom, they joined a God-glorifying battle for

Thomas Lewis Johnson

National Portrait Gallery, Smithsonian Institution

the acknowledgment of their dignity. Where they wrote down their testimonies, I want to share their testimonies with readers who deserve to know their accomplishments. Where they had not the power of the pen, I want to write their words for them.

Read.

10

"The Rights Which Manhood Can Confer"

The myths of Reconstruction would live well past the ending of the period, despite the reliable primary source documents that tell the truth about the period. Many of those myths derive from a movie that shaped much of the American imagination around the Civil War and Reconstruction—*The Birth of a Nation*. And the best stage to refute the outright fantasy D. W. Griffith presents is that of the debates over the Civil Rights Bill of 1875.

> We do not fear censorship, for we have no wish to offend with improprieties or obscenities, but we do demand, as a right, the liberty to show the dark side of wrong, that we may illuminate the bright side of virtue—the same liberty that is conceded to the art of the written word—that art to which we owe the Bible and the works of Shakespeare.[1]

D. W. Griffith spoke these words in the wake of his controversial epoch *The Birth of a Nation*. While history often remembers the mammoth impact of his film (which was shown at the White House[2]), it less often recalls the massive blowback and criticism at the time of its release. The silent three-hour saga was like *The Lord of the Rings* for the Progressive Era. The reviews were overwhelmingly positive, relaying the slack-jawed audience's wonder at Griffith's masterpiece.

But they weren't *all* positive.

One activist, William Monroe Trotter, went head-to-head with Griffith in the historic town of Boston. He and a group of protesters "descended on the Tremont Theater" and kicked up such a fuss that they disrupted ticket sales.[3] Across America, Black activists spoke out against the film and advocated for its banning. The criticism grew so intense that Griffith wrote a tome dedicated to defending his right to free speech: *The Rise and Fall of Free Speech in America*. His tirade lambasted censorship as the fruit of intolerance. And intolerance is, after all, what crucified Christ.

Griffith reminded his readers that his was a noble cause—to teach *history*. "Fortunes are spent every year in our country in teaching the truth of history," he stated, and now, that history was to be taught outside of colleges and universities in movie theaters.

> The foremost educators of the country have urged upon us moving picture producers to put away the slap-stick comedies, the ridiculous, sentimental "mush" stories, the imitation of the cheap magazines, and go to the fields of history for our subjects. They have told us repeatedly that the motion picture can impress upon a people as much of the truth of history in an evening as many months of study will accomplish. As one eminent divine has said to the masses, "It teaches history by lightning." We would like very much to do this.[4]

Trotter's protestations, according to Griffith, were rooted in intolerance and a denial of historical testimony. Even worse, they wore the mask of reform while stemming from the worst type of intolerance: intolerance toward what Griffith considered the truth of history.

Most modern viewers would not make it through the three-hour tale that is *Birth of a Nation*. But those who do will encounter some of the mainstays of Confederate propaganda: happy slaves shucking and jiving for their masters, noble Confederate soldiers defending the virtue of their women, and Southerners victimized by Northern carpetbaggers in the wake of the Civil War.

One of the most interesting scenes takes place in the latter part of the film. Before the clip, a slide explains:

> The negro party in control of the State House of Representatives, 101 blacks against 23 whites, session of 1871.
> An historical facsimile of the State House of Representatives of South Carolina as it was in 1870. After photograph by Columbia State.

The next clip shows Black legislators gathered to deliberate, some of them Black men and others white men in blackface. They are raucous, sneaking whiskey bottles from jacket pockets, eating chicken legs in the middle of the meeting, and reclining with their feet on their desks. After one member kicks off his boots and wiggles his bare toes in the middle of the session, a slide quips, "The speaker rules that all members must wear shoes."

The film records two other motions:

1. It is moved and carried that all whites must salute negro officers in the streets.
2. Passage of a bill, providing the intermarriage of Blacks and whites.

When the second bill is passed, the Black representatives leer up at the white women in the wings of the legislative floor,

185

foreshadowing the impending death of a white woman who pitches herself off the side of a mountain rather than submitting to the touch of the Black man who wishes to marry her.

That "Black" man (a white man in blackface) is tried and executed by the Ku Klux Klan before being thrown onto the porch of the lieutenant governor.

This is the "history" Griffith's diatribe defends.

This is the "history" Trotter protested to such a degree that he made enemies all the way to the White House.

Black Congressmen

The long-term results of Griffith's groundbreaking film vary. If modern students *do* have thoughts about the Reconstruction, they view it as a failed experiment that left white Southerners disenfranchised and embittered toward the powers that be. Perhaps they have a passing thought about Black congressmen

THE FIFTEENTH AMENDMENT.
CELEBRATED MAY 19T 1870

Harry T. Peters "America on Stone" Lithography Collection

186

who were given too much responsibility too soon and tanked Southern economy and culture with far-reaching effects.

Most likely, though, they are unaware of the fact that more than 1,500 Black officeholders were elected during Reconstruction, that 185 of them held federal offices, and that sixteen of them were congressmen.

When the Civil War ended and the Thirteenth, Fourteenth, and Fifteenth Amendments were passed, Black men were allowed suffrage in every state for the first time in American history. In some Southern counties, the formerly enslaved outnumbered their white counterparts, and as a result, they were able to vote for Black candidates who had their best interest at heart.

Currier and Ives produced an 1872 lithograph called "The First Colored Senator and Representatives." In it, Senator Hiram Revels and Representatives Benjamin Turner, Robert De Large, Josiah Walls, Jefferson Long, Joseph Rainey, and

The first colored senator and representatives—in the 41st and 42nd Congress of the United States: Top left to right, Robert C. De Large, Jefferson H. Long; bottom, H. R. Revels, Benj. S. Turner, Josiah T. Walls, Joseph H. Rainy [i.e., Rainey], and R. Brown Elliot

Robert B. Elliot are assembled, cutting impressive figures in three-piece suits, refined carriage, and fashionable facial hair. Their image could not be further from the brutish, lazy, morally degenerate, and dangerous minstrelsy portrayed in *The Birth of a Nation*. Though five of the seven men were born into slavery, every single one of them rose to become an important figure in the political mechanizations of Reconstruction—and contrary to Griffith's portrayal, "intermarriage" was not at the top of their list of concerns.

They were, however, concerned with the Civil Rights Act of 1875.

Yet another important measure often lost to history, this act was proposed by radical Republican Charles Sumner. The congressman had made a name for himself as an anti-slavery advocate back in the 1850s. When Kansas was admitted into the Union, Sumner argued against allowing slavery in the state, leveling pointed jabs at two pro-slavery senators, Stephen Douglas and Andrew Butler.

"He characterized Douglas to his face as a 'noise-some, squat, and nameless animal . . . not a proper model for an American senator.'"[5] But he reserved his most scathing critique for Andrew Butler, who was not in attendance on that day in May 1856:

> The senator from South Carolina has read many books of chivalry, and believes himself a chivalrous knight, with sentiments of honor and courage. Of course he has chosen a mistress to whom he has made his vows, and who, though ugly to others, is always lovely to him; though polluted in the sight of the world, is chaste in his sight—I mean the harlot, slavery.[6]

Representative Preston Brooks, also from South Carolina, waited until the Senate adjourned for the day, then calmly walked up to Sumner and beat him with a cane. A bloody Sumner was carried off for medical attention while Brooks strode coolly out of the Senate chamber without repercussion for his violence.

If the threat of bodily harm was still on Sumner's mind during his campaigning for the Civil Rights Act, he did not show it. He died before the act was voted upon.

> Sumner predicted that the Civil Rights Act would be the greatest achievement of Reconstruction. "Very few measures of equal importance have ever been presented," he proclaimed. Unfortunately, Sumner did not live to see the fate of his bill. He died of a heart attack in 1874—just 63 years old. "Don't let the bill fail," the dying Sumner pleaded to Frederick Douglass and others at his bedside. "You must take care of [my] civil rights bill."[7]

Alexander H. Stephens, former vice president of the Confederacy and one of the most vocal opponents of the bill, had been convicted of treason only a few years prior and served a five-month prison sentence before being elected as a senator in Georgia. Stephens was set to debate the Civil Rights bill with South Carolina representative Robert B. Elliott on January 6, 1874.

By the time Elliott stepped onto the senate floor that fateful day, newspapers were abuzz. He represented an anomaly in the Reconstruction era, as a dark-skinned Black man with clout.

Many of the well-known names of the era, including Elliott's fellow congressmen, were the children of slaveholders and enslaved women. In some cases, their proximity to whiteness through their father allowed them to achieve a level of education and independence before the Civil War. Frederick Douglass, Booker T. Washington, and W. E. B. Du Bois could all trace their lineage to slaveholders, Douglass and Washington directly through their fathers. Some commentators of the period surmised that the intelligence of these men was due to their proximity to whiteness. Of *course* Frederick Douglass was well-spoken for a Black man—he got it from his white father. Yes, Du Bois was a brilliant thinker—it came from his French ancestry.

Photo Montage (1876), Library of Congress

Elliott had no such white ancestry—at least, no such white ancestry that was immediately apparent. He had been born of Caribbean immigrants, raised and educated in England, and built a career as a lawyer. When he stood toe-to-toe with Stephens, the watching world was stripped of its excuses for this Black man's prowess.[8]

On that January day, Robert B. Elliott squared his shoulders and delivered a stirring speech denouncing the racism of former vice president Alexander H. Stephens:

> Sir, it is scarcely twelve years since that gentleman shocked the civilized world by announcing the birth of a government which rested on human slavery as its corner-stone. The progress of

events has swept away that pseudo-government which rested on greed, pride, and tyranny; and the race who he then ruthlessly spurned and tramped on are here to meet him in debate, and to demand that the rights which are enjoyed by their former oppressors—who vainly sought to overthrow a Government for which they could not prostitute to the base uses of slavery—shall be accorded to those who even in the darkness of slavery kept their allegiance to freedom and the Union. Sir, the gentleman from Georgia has learned much since 1861; but he is still a laggard. Let him put away the entirely false and fatal theories which have so greatly marred an otherwise enviable record. **Let him accept, in its fullness and beneficence, the great doctrine that American citizenship carries with it every civil and political right which manhood can confer.** Let him lend his influence, with all masterly ability, to complete the proud structure of legislation which makes this nation worthy of the great declaration which heralded its birth, and he will have done that which will most nearly redeem his reputation in the eyes of the world, and best vindicate the wisdom of that policy which has permitted him to regain his seat upon this floor.[9]

Elliott hearkened back to Alexander Stephen's famous Cornerstone Speech, which, if you'll remember, stated:

Our new government is founded upon exactly the opposite idea; its foundations are laid, its corner-stone rests, upon the great truth that the negro is not equal to the white man; that slavery subordination to the superior race is his natural and normal condition. This, our new government, is the first, in the history of the world, based upon this great physical, philosophical, and moral truth.[10]

In case his listeners forgot, Elliott reminded them of Stephens's treasonous bid to "overthrow a Government for which they could not prostitute to the base use of slavery."[11] He used strong language to remind his hearers of the heinousness of

slavery's existence in this new Republic. Stephens may have learned a few things since 1861, Elliott allowed, "but he is still a laggard." He dressed down Stephens while offering him a way forward: accept the extension of American citizenship to Black Americans—accept this citizenship has made America "worthy of the great declaration which heralded its birth"—and his reputation would be redeemed.

Of course, Stephens would accept no such olive branch. But the civil rights bill *did* pass. And it required

> that all persons within the jurisdiction of the United States shall be entitled to the full and equal enjoyment of the accommodations, advantages, facilities, and privileges of inns, public conveyances on land or water, theaters, and other places of public amusement; subject only to the conditions and limitations established by law, and applicable alike to citizens of every race and color, regardless of any previous condition of servitude.[12]

192

Notably, the "intermarriage of blacks and whites," as D. W. Griffith put it, was not on the table.

In fact, Representative Joseph H. Rainey said:

> We do not ask it of you, we do not ask of the gentleman from Kentucky that the two races should intermarry one with the other. God knows we are perfectly content. I can say for myself that I am contented to be what I am so long as I have my rights; I am contented to marry one of my own complexion, and do not seek intercourse with any other race, because I believe that the race of people I represent, to the extent of the opportunities which they have had, and considering how recently they have escaped from the oppression and wrongs committed upon them, are just as virtuous and hold just as many high characteristics as any class in the country. I think the statistics will prove that there is as much virtue among the negroes as among the whites.

Rainey wanted his listeners to know he was not advocating "the passage of any law forcing us upon anybody who does not want to receive us." Rather, he called for full citizenship under the law, one that had already been promised in the Fourteenth and Fifteenth Amendments to the Constitution. He also held those assembled accountable to their own liberty documents in the same manner as Robert B. Elliott:

> I say to you gentlemen, that this discrimination against the negro race in this country is unjust, is unworthy of a high-minded people whose example should have a salutary influence in the world.[13]

Richard H. Cain ended his speech in favor of the Civil Rights Act, not just appealing to the United States government, but to God as well:

> Our wives and our children have high hopes and aspirations; their longings for manhood and womanhood are equal to those

of any other race. The same sentiment of patriotism and of gratitude, the same spirit of national pride that animates the hearts of other citizens, animates theirs. In the name of the dead soldiers of our race, whose bodies lie at Petersburgh and on other battle-fields of the South; in the name of the widows and orphans they have left behind; in the name of the widows of the confederate soldiers who fell upon the same fields, I conjure you let this righteous act be done. I appeal to you in the name of God and humanity to give us our rights, for we ask nothing more.

If these words sound a bit like a benediction, it's because Richard H. Cain was an AME minister appointed by none other than Bishop Daniel Payne. His theological groundwork peeked out again when he quipped:

We believe that God Almighty has made of one blood all the nations upon the face of the earth. We believe we are made just like white men are. [Laughter.] Look; I stretch out my arms. See; I have two of them, as you have. Look at your ears; I have two of them. I have two eyes, two nostrils, one mouth, two feet. I stand erect like you. I am clothed with humanity like you. I think, I reason, I talk, I express my views, as you do. Is there any difference between us? Not so far as our manhood is concerned. Unless it be in this: That our opinions differ, and mine are a little higher up than yours.[14]

What would it be like to hear these words spoken over D. W. Griffith's senate chamber scene? Instead of the music providing the background for this silent film, what if Black voices declared their humanity while the actors on the screen clowned around in front of the camera?

What would it have been like to watch a 1915 film that portrayed these proceedings with the dignity of that Currier and Ives lithograph? Would *that* be like "writing history with lightning," terribly, awe-inspiringly true?

Pirate Senator

Some senators left behind their stirring legacies in the speeches they gave. Others, like Robert Smalls, left an enduring legacy in other ways.

Smalls was born into slavery in Beaufort, South Carolina, in 1839. When he was sixteen, he was allowed to work in Charleston for sixteen dollars a week. His enslaver kept most of his earnings, but Smalls was given one dollar to save each week. His work in Charleston centered around the harbors, which would be an important ingredient to his future liberation.

In 1861, Smalls gathered his wife, their children, and several slaves willing to take the risk and told them about his daring plan of escape. Two enslaved men opted to stay behind for fear the plan would fail.

At two o'clock in the morning on May 13, Smalls set sail. He was likely the son of his enslaver, and as such, could be confused for a white man at a distance. He donned the straw hat normally worn by the captain of the cotton steamer the *Planter*, impersonating him and *stealing his boat* to sail toward the Union blockade. They sailed with a hull full of dynamite: if caught by the Confederacy, they would choose to die in a fiery explosion rather than face the wrath of the South.

Instead, they nearly faced the wrath of the North.

As they neared the blockade, the rebel flag signaled aggression to the Union soldiers.

In *The Negro's Civil War*, the dean of Civil War studies James McPherson quotes the following eyewitness account: "Just as No. 3 port gun was being elevated, someone cried out, 'I see something that looks like a white flag'; and true enough there was something flying on the steamer that would have been *white* by application of soap and water. As she neared us, we looked in vain for the face of a white man. When they discovered that we would not fire on them, there was a rush of contrabands out on her deck, some dancing, some singing, whistling, jumping; and others stood looking towards Fort Sumter, and muttering all sorts of maledictions against it, and *'de heart of de Souf,'* generally. As the steamer came near, and under the stern of the *Onward,* one of the Colored men stepped forward, and taking off his hat, shouted, 'Good morning, sir! I've brought you some of the old United States guns, sir!'" That man is Robert Smalls, and he and his family and the entire slave crew of the *Planter* are now free.[15]

The Confederates were confounded. Even though they acknowledged Smalls's complicity in the piracy (a $4,000 bounty was put on his head), they did not understand how a Black man and his Black compatriots could have pulled off the stunt. Such cunning was seen as far above the capacity of an enslaved man no matter who his father was.

Once free, Smalls personally petitioned Secretary of War Edwin Stanton to allow Black men into the Union Army. He recruited 5,000 Black troops himself, according to historian Henry Louis Gates, and fought on the sea until the end of the war, earn-

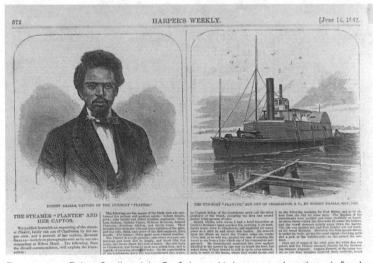

Future senator Robert Smalls and the Confederate ship he commandeered to gain freedom

ing himself the rank of captain. Afterward, he bought the house where he had been enslaved and died there on February 22, 1915, exactly two weeks after the release of *The Birth of a Nation.*

Death of Progress

In 1883, the Supreme Court ruled the Civil Rights Act of 1875 unconstitutional. As the gains of Reconstruction were rolled back, senators like Robert B. Elliott and Robert Smalls found reelection impossible. Black voters once again became disenfranchised, and the system of slavery was replaced with Jim Crow, a litany of rules and regulations that kept Black Southerners "in check."

The next Black Southerner to lead as a representative from South Carolina would be Tim Scott in 2003.

In 1896, *Plessy v. Ferguson* upheld the "separate but equal" doctrine of segregation, although there was nothing equal about the segregation of the South. The story of the Civil War was recast, not as a Southern battle to uphold and expand slavery, but as a Southern battle for nebulous "states' rights" fought by Confederate soldiers cast as the true patriots fighting in the spirit of their colonial ancestors.

As the progress of Reconstruction died a slow and painful death, the landscape of Black activism began to change form.

In 1895, both W. E. B. Du Bois and William Monroe Trotter graduated from Harvard, Frederick Douglass died, and Booker T. Washington was poised to take the giant's place as the most vocal leader of Black Americans.

In a speech that same year, Washington showed his hand. With the *Plessy* decision looming on the horizon, he wanted his listeners to focus on things more important than desegregation. He warned the Black man:

> Cast it down in agriculture, mechanics, in commerce, in domestic service, and in the professions. . . . Our greatest danger is

that in the great leap from slavery to freedom we may overlook the fact that the masses of us are to live by the productions of our hands, and fail to keep in mind that we shall prosper in proportion as we learn to dignify and glorify common labour, and put brains and skill into the common occupations of life.

Washington wanted his Black listeners to understand that the golden years of the Reconstruction were over. Equality with the white man and suffrage were not goals Black men should be focused on. Instead, they should devote themselves to building their communities, their monetary and social capital, and their skill.

A few breaths later, he assured the white man their families would be surrounded by the most patient, faithful, law-abiding, and unresentful people the world has seen.

As we have proved our loyalty to you in the past, in nursing your children, watching by the sick-bed of your mothers and fathers, and often following them with tear-dimmed eyes to their graves, so in the future, in our humble way, we shall stand by you with a devotion that no foreigner can approach, ready to lay down our lives, if need be, in defense of yours, interlacing our industrial, commercial, civil, and religious life with yours in a way that shall make the interests of both races one. In all things that are purely social we can be as separate as the fingers, yet one as the hand in all things essential to mutual progress.

Washington's speech was a runaway success—and not just with white benefactors. Certainly, it appealed to paternalistic white people who wanted nothing more than to hear a Black man promise to stay in his place and work very hard. But to say these were the *only* people and the *only* reasons the speech resonated would be to oversimplify the issue. Washington was speaking in Atlanta and had set up a trade school in the South. He knew intimately what a fight for equality in the Jim Crow era would entail. And, in his estimation, that equality wasn't as important as industry.

He was speaking to a group of people one generation removed from slavery. He himself spoke as a formerly enslaved man educated in the postwar South by the Freedman's Bureau. These formerly enslaved people had not received reparations. They were starting from scratch and trying to build generational wealth. Washington felt it was important for them to "tend their own garden" before worrying about how the white man would receive them. He believed that if everyone put their nose to the grindstone and worked for the success of the nation, the other issues would take care of themselves.

> That higher good . . . let us pray God, will come, in a blotting out of sectional differences and racial animosities and suspicions, in a determination to administer absolute justice, in a willing obedience among all classes to the mandates of law. This, coupled with our material prosperity, will bring into our beloved South a new heaven and a new earth.[16]

Trotter vehemently disagreed, having made it his life's mission to pursue the equal rights that Black Americans were still being denied. His newspaper's motto was "For every right with all thy might."

Booker T. Washington died in November of 1915, several months after *The Birth of a Nation* premiered in theaters. One could argue that he contributed much more to the cause of Black Americans than the boycotting of a film. He founded the Tuskegee Institute and the National Negro Business League. He helped secure donations for Black education and served as an adviser to both Presidents William McKinley and Theodore Roosevelt. And quietly as it's kept, he fought against segregation with his money, which he earned with the same philosophy he promoted, secretly financing lawsuits to "block attempts to disfranchise and segregate" Black Americans.[17]

In fact, "since his death in 1915, historians have discovered voluminous private correspondence that shows that Washington's apparent conservatism was only part of his strategy for uplifting his race."[18] He was the poster child for collecting more flies with honey than with vinegar, landing big donors like Andrew Carnegie to his public causes while using his own funds to finance the causes he claimed were distractions from valuable community uplift.

Even though Trotter is on record responding to *The Birth of a Nation*, it's simple to guess what Washington might have said about it in public . . . and in private. Publicly: let white Southerners feel proud of their heritage, and let's work doubly hard to ensure that those caricatures look as ridiculous as possible next to our success.

Privately?

He might have cheered Trotter's boycott on and slipped a few dollars to the cause.

A Different Kind of Story

In 1920, Oscar Micheaux, the first Black filmmaker to produce full-length films, directed *Within Our Gates*. Its budget was nowhere near *The Birth of a Nation*'s, and its runtime is short by comparison. But Micheaux was a Black storyteller committed to telling the truth about the Jim Crow violence of the South.

Unlike *The Birth of a Nation*, Micheaux's film is set in contemporary times and follows a Black schoolteacher taking part in the Great Migration. Like *The Birth of a Nation*, it features the KKK and a lynching; unlike *The Birth of a Nation*, neither is glorified. *Within Our Gates* was even banned in certain places, and when it was shown, some scenes were cut to appeal to certain audiences' sensibilities.

America was coming off the Red Summer of 1919, a time of widespread racial violence where white supremacist terrorism reached a peak, resulting in at least twelve race riots (more accurately called massacres, as most of the victims were Black) across the country. This violence was in reaction to several tensions: Black soldiers were returning from World War I and threatening notions of white supremacy. The Great Migration was also occurring. Fleeing the violence of the Jim Crow South, Southern Blacks migrated in droves to the North, and not everyone was responding favorably to the changes. Red Summer revealed that racism wasn't just a Southern problem—it was an American problem.

Critics worried that this backdrop would make Micheaux's film a powder keg.

And yet, he still told the truth.

His film humanized those *The Birth of a Nation* dehumanized. It gave dignity to those *The Birth of a Nation* scoffed at. It took the violent imagery of *The Birth of a Nation* and mourned it rather than celebrating it.

Micheaux went on to make over forty-four films, becoming an important artistic voice during the Harlem Renaissance, which produced a bevy of other truth-telling artists: Langston Hughes, Claude McCay, Zora Neale Hurston, Nella Larsen, and others. The Jessie Fauset era of *The Crisis*—the official magazine of the NAACP, which was founded in 1910 by W. E. B. Du Bois—was also in full swing. During her tenure as editor, Fauset brought more and more artistic voices into the publication, helping to fuel the Renaissance.

Black voices abounded.

Unlike D. W. Griffith, these Black artists *did* have reason to fear censorship.

Some of their work is still in danger of being censored at the time of this writing.

But like D. W. Griffith, they wrote with the confidence that they were telling the unapologetic truth, "illuminating the bright side of virtue," as they declared their humanity both explicitly and implicitly.

History makes clear who handled fellow image bearers with the most care.

AFTERWORD

In the writing of this book, my editors and I often joked that there were *so many quotes*.

Throughout the editing process, one of the most common notes was, "Can you expand on this more in your own words?"

It was an overcorrection to a problem that occurs so often in telling the stories of resistance to slavery: center on outside commentary and not the stories of those who were *there*.

It is important to let the enslaved and the objectors to enslavement speak for themselves for several reasons.

First, so often, when looking at the history of enslavement, readers tend to look at the perspective of the oppressor first. When laymen ask questions like, "Did anyone know that slavery was wrong?" they are generally referring to "anyone" as "any white person who might have benefited from slavery" and not "anyone" as "any Black person who might have been in bondage." (Although both white and Black Americans testified to the brutality of slavery.)

When people ask, "Did anyone in the church stand up for the rights of the enslaved?" they generally mean, "Did any white churchmen stand up for the rights of the enslaved?"[1] They don't usually mean, "What was the Black church saying about slavery?" because the Black church isn't at the center of their understanding of what the American church is.

To ask what Black men and women thought about slavery—both those in chains and those outside the chains—is to center the oppressed in our conversation about oppression. And, outside the academy, that's not something many tend to get right.

Second, it is far less important for me to wax eloquent about my ideals of the *imago Dei* than to show you that those ideals have been built on the foundation of the Christians who came before me—the Black Christians who came before me. I share these words to point out that they are part of a robust legacy that has so often been forgotten and obscured by focusing our historical inquiry on the oppressor instead of looking at the fruit so often borne by the oppressed. The enslaved had a well-rounded theology of suffering and victory in Christ that modern Christians would do well to learn from and emulate.

I have already written a book about how the stories of women from the past empowered me—in *Carved in Ebony*'s pages, my story is very much a present and active part of the reader's experience. In this book, though, I wanted to step out of the way and let the stories speak for themselves. Will these pages inspire you in your own life? Absolutely. Have they inspired me in mine? Most assuredly. But the inspiration isn't the central facet of the story we're telling here, because even that inspiration can center our experience of history more than the important history itself. And that is never my intention.

Finally, as a Christian, it's very important for me to communicate that the saving faith of Christ has *always* borne fruit in this country. But when modern-day Christians are constantly looking for that fruit in the lives of enslavers and oppressors, they are shaking the wrong trees. The gospel fruit borne by those who stood against the widespread practice of chattel slavery is far sweeter. And its evidence is abundantly clear in the testimonies that these men and women left behind—we just haven't been looking for them. Or rather, we've been looking in the wrong places. The testimonies in this book are my effort to steer us to look in the right places.

The fact that these testimonies were left behind *despite* a culture that tried to render the enslaved illiterate and unable to share those testimonies? That's an act of God.

I tried to follow my editor's wise direction and put in more commentary, so that you didn't just read walls of nineteenth-century text and quotes (though books like that have their place). I wanted to steer the story so that you could have a framework for just how amazing it is. But I also wanted it to be clear that my job is to get out of the way and let the truth shine bright.

So, I wrote you an afterword with not a quote in sight.

It was a feat, I assure you.

NOTES

Introduction

1. bell hooks, *Teaching to Transgress* (New York: Routledge, 1994), 2, 3.

2. LaGarrett J. King, "When Lions Write History: Black History Textbooks, African-American Educators, & the Alternative Black Curriculum in Social Studies Education, 1890–1940," *Multicultural Education* 22, no. 1 (Fall 2014): 2–11, https://eric.ed.gov/?id=EJ1065311.

3. Edward A. Johnson, *A School History of the Negro Race in America* (Chicago: Isaac Goldman Co. Printers, 1895), iii.

4. Leila Amos Pendleton, *A Narrative of the Negro* (Washington, DC: Press of R.L. Pendleton, 1912), 3.

5. Pendleton, *Narrative of the Negro*, 63.

6. LaGarrett J. King, "'A Narrative to the Colored Children in America': Lelia Amos Pendleton, African American History Textbooks, and Challenging Personhood," *Journal of Negro Education* 84, no. 4 (2015): 519–33, https://doi.org/10.7709/jnegroeducation.84.4.0519.

7. Chara Bohan, interview with Jennifer Rainey Marquez, "Rewriting History," Georgia State University *Research Magazine*, https://news.gsu.edu/research-magazine/rewriting-history-civil-war-textbooks.

8. James Baldwin, *Notes of a Native Son* (Boston: Beacon, 2012), 10, Kindle edition.

Chapter One Give Me Liberty

1. Nat Turner, *The Confessions of Nat Turner, The Leader of the Late Insurrection in Southampton, VA* (Baltimore: Thomas R. Gray, 1830), 10, https://docsouth.unc.edu/neh/turner/turner.html.

2. *Encyclopedia of Southern Culture*, ed. Charles Reagan Wilson and William Ferris, s.v. "Turner, Nat (1800–1831) Slave" (Chapel Hill: University of North Carolina Press, 1989), in Documenting the American South, https://docsouth.unc.edu/neh/turner/bio.html.

3. Turner, *Confessions of Nat Turner*, 10.

4. Turner, 11.

5. Moses Coit Tyler, *American Statesman: Patrick Henry* (Boston: Houghton Mifflin, 1898), https://play.google.com/books/reader?id=saBBAAAAYAAJ&pg=GBS.PR12&hl=en.

6. Patrick Henry, "Give Me Liberty or Give Me Death" (speech, Virginia Convention, March 23, 1775), https://avalon.law.yale.edu/18th_century/patrick.asp.

7. Tyler, *American Statesman*.

8. David Walker, *Walker's Appeal, in Four Articles; Together with a Preamble, to the Coloured Citizens of the World, but in Particular, and Very Expressly, to Those of the United States of America* (Boston: David Walker, 1830), 19, https://docsouth.unc.edu/nc/walker/walker.html.

9. Walker, 12.

10. Nell Irvin Painter, *History of White People* (New York: W. W. Norton, 2010), 144.

11. Thomas Jefferson, *Notes on the State of Virginia* (Philadelphia: Richard & Hall, 1785), 148, https://docsouth.unc.edu/southlit/jefferson/jefferson.html.

12. Harlow G. Unger, *Lion of Liberty: Patrick Henry and the Call to a New Nation* (Cambridge, MA: Da Capo Press, 2011), 238, Kindle edition.

13. Steven Mintz, "Historical Context: American Slavery in Comparative Perspective," The Gilder Lehrman Institute of American History, https://www.gilderlehrman.org/history-resources/teaching-resource/historical-context-american-slavery-comparative-perspective.

14. Greg Timmons, "How Slavery Became the Economic Engine of the South," The History Channel, September 2, 2020, https://www.history.com/news/slavery-profitable-southern-economy#:~:text=Archives%2FGetty%20Images-,Slavery%20was%20so%20profitable%2C%20it%20sprouted%20more%20millionaires%20per%20capita,engine%20of%20the%20burgeoning%20nation.

15. Francis Ellen Harper, "Liberty for Slaves," 1857, https://www.blackpast.org/african-american-history/1857-frances-ellen-watkins-liberty-slaves/.

16. The Naturalization Act of 1790 limited citizenship to "free white person[s] . . . of good character."

17. Walker, *Appeal*, 20.

18. Walker, 73.

19. Walker, 71.

20. Walker, 6.

21. Holly Jackson, *American Radicals* (New York: Crown, 2019), 61, Kindle edition.

22. Jefferson, *Notes on the State of Virginia*, 147.

23. Thomas Jefferson, letter from Monticello, April 22, 1820, https://www.loc.gov/exhibits/jefferson/159.html.

24. Frederick Douglass, *Life of an American Slave* (Boston: Anti-Slavery Office, 1845), appendix, http://utc.iath.virginia.edu/abolitn/abaufda14t.html.

25. James Baldwin, "6 James Baldwin Quotes about Race," *American Masters*, PBS, August 4, 2020, https://www.pbs.org/wnet/americanmasters/6-james-baldwin-quotes-race/15142/.

26. Pendleton, *Narrative of the Negro*, 116.

27. Edward A. Johnson, *A School History of the Negro Race in America from 1619 to 1890* (Chicago: WB Conkey Company, 1895), 92.

28. The year that the first slave ship arrived at Jamestown.

Chapter Two A Double Victory

1. "L," "The Liberator," Revisiting Rebellion: Nat Turner in the American Imagination, https://americanantiquarian.org/NatTurner/the-liberator.

2. William Lloyd Garrison, address delivered at Malboro Chapel, 1838, https://archive.org/stream/addressdeliver00garris/addressdeliver00garris_djvu.txt.

3. Robert J. Breckinridge, *Hints on Slavery* (Lexington, KY: n.p., 1843), https://archive.org/details/hintsonslavery00brec/page/16/mode/2up.

4. James Forten, *Letters from a Man of Colour, on a Late Bill before the Senate of Pennsylvania*, The Gilder Lehrman Institute of American History, https://www.gilderlehrman.org/collection/glc06046.

5. Robert Breckinridge, "Hints on Colonization and Abolition; with Reference to the Black Race," *Biblical Repertory*, no. 3 (July 1833), https://static1.squarespace.com/static/590be125ff7c502a07752a5b/t/5df00cdcf9cd7913d3282f9d/1576013022510/Breckinridge%2C+Robert+Jefferson%2C+Hints+on+Colonization+and+Abolition.pdf.

6. "American Colonization Society, 1816–1865," Africans in America, https://www.pbs.org/wgbh/aia/part3/3p1521.html.

7. Breckinridge, "Hints on Colonization and Abolition."

8. Haroon Kharem, "Chapter Four: The American Colonization Society," *Counterpoints* 208 (2006): 75–101, http://www.jstor.org/stable/42980005.

9. Kharem, "Chapter Four."

10. *Herald of Freedom*, March 16, 1839, vol. 5, issue 3.

11. Sarah Forten, *Speak Out in Thunder Tones: Letters and Other Writings by Black Northerners, 1787–1865*, ed. Dorothy Sterling (Boston: Da Capo Press, 1998), 56.

12. *Herald of Freedom*, March 16, 1839.

13. Julie Winch, *A Gentleman of Color: The Life of James Forten* (New York: Oxford University Press, 2002), loc. 4673–76, Kindle edition.

14. Julie Winch, "'You Know I Am a Man of Business': James Forten and the Factor of Race in Philadelphia's Antebellum Business Community,"

Business and Economic History 26, no. 1 (1997): 213–28, http://www.jstor.org/stable/23703308.

15. Winch, "'Man of Business.'"

16. Charles A. Simmons, *The African American Press: A History of News Coverage During National Crises, with Special Reference to Four Black Newspapers, 1827–1965* (Jefferson, NC: McFarland, 1998), 80.

17. Olivia B. Waxman, "How a 1946 Case of Police Brutality against a Black WWII Veteran Shaped the Fight for Civil Rights," *Time*, March 30, 2021, https://time.com/5950641/blinding-isaac-woodard/.

Chapter Three The Double Curse

1. "A Young Lady of Color," *Liberator*, May 11, 1833, https://libraries.ud mercy.edu/archives/special-collections/index.php?collectionCode=baa&rec ord_id=2168&item_id=2536.

2. Sarah Forten Purvis, "The Slave Girl's Address to Her Mother," Better Days, 2020, https://www.utahwomenshistory.org/wp-content/uploads/2019 /01/Sarah-Forten-Purvis%E2%80%99s-poem.pdf.

3. James Redpath, *The Roving Editor* (New York: AB Burdick Publisher, 1852), 42.

4. Barbara Welter, "The Cult of True Womanhood: 1820–1860," *American Quarterly* 18, no. 2 (1966): 151–74, https://doi.org/10.2307/2711179.

5. Carolyn A. Day, *Consumptive Chic* (New York: Bloomsbury, 2020), 2–3, Kindle edition.

6. Thomas Branagan, *The Excellency of the Female Character Vindicated Being an Investigation Relative to the Cause and Effects of the Encroachments of Men upon the Rights of Women, and the Too Frequent Degradation and Consequent Misfortunes of the Fair Sex* (Philadelphia: J. Rakestraw, 1808), 123.

7. Ruby Hamad, *White Tears/Brown Scars: How White Feminism Betrays Women of Color* (New York: Catapult, 2020), 24, Kindle edition.

8. Wilma King, *The Essence of Liberty: Free Black Women during the Slave Era* (Columbia: University of Missouri Press), 42.

9. William Summers, artist; Charles Hunt, engraver, "The Lub Letter," Life in Philadelphia no. 4 (London: G.S. Tregear, c. 1833), https://digital.lib rarycompany.org/islandora/object/Islandora%3A60232.

10. Brent Tarter, "Elizabeth Key (fl. 1655–1660)," *Dictionary of Virginia Biography*, Library of Virginia, 2019, https://www.lva.virginia.gov/public /dvb/bio.php?b=Key_Elizabeth_fl_1655-1660.

11. Jonathan L. Alpert, "The Origin of Slavery in the United States—The Maryland Precedent," *American Journal of Legal History* 14, no. 3 (1970): 189–221, https://doi.org/10.2307/844413.

12. Maria W. Stewart, "Why Sit Ye Here and Die?" (lecture, Franklin Hall, Boston, September 21, 1832), https://awpc.cattcenter.iastate.edu/2020/11/20 /why-sit-ye-here-and-die-sept-21-1832/.

13. Jackson, *American Radicals*, 6, Kindle edition.
14. Margaret Hope Bacon, "'The Double Curse of Sex and Color': Robert Purvis and Human Rights," *Pennsylvania Magazine of History and Biography* 121, no. 1/2 (1997): 53–76, http://www.jstor.org/stable/20093103.
15. Winch, *Gentleman of Color*, loc. 6222–24, Kindle edition.
16. Shirley Yee, *Black Women Abolitionists: A Study in Activism, 1828–1860* (Knoxville: University of Tennessee Press, 1992), 42.
17. Yee, *Black Women Abolitionists*, 46.
18. Chloe Spear, *Memoir of Mrs. Chloe Spear, A Native of Africa, Who Was Enslaved in Childhood, and Died in Boston, January 3, 1815 . . . Aged 65 Years* (Boston: James Loring, 1832), https://docsouth.unc.edu/neh/brownrw /brownrw.html.
19. "The Other Rosa Parks: Now 73, Claudette Colvin Was First to Refuse Giving Up Seat on Montgomery Bus," video, Democracy Now!, March 29, 2013, https://www.democracynow.org/2013/3/29/the_other_rosa_parks _now_73.
20. Jeanne Theoharris, "Claudette Colvin," *The Rebellious Life of Mrs. Rosa Parks*, https://rosaparksbiography.org/bio/claudette-colvin/.
21. Margaret Hope Bacon, "'One Great Bundle of Humanity': Frances Ellen Watkins Harper (1825–1911)," *Pennsylvania Magazine of History and Biography* 113, no. 1 (1989): 21–43, http://www.jstor.org/stable/2009 2281.

Chapter Four "Marriage under Such a System"

1. Emily Hessney, "Lydia Maria Child to Harriet Jacobs Letter," River Campus Libraries, December 3, 2008, https://rbscp.lib.rochester.edu/4446.
2. Stephanie M. H. Camp, *Closer to Freedom: Enslaved Women and Everyday Resistance in the Plantation South*, Gender and American Culture (Chapel Hill: University of North Carolina Press, 2004), 104, Kindle edition.
3. *Webster's Dictionary 1828*, s.v. "amalgamation," https://webstersdiction ary1828.com/Dictionary/amalgamation.
4. Camp, *Closer to Freedom*, 112, Kindle edition.
5. Harriet A. Jacobs, *Incidents in the Life of a Slave Girl* (Boston: Jacobs, 1861), 83, https://docsouth.unc.edu/fpn/jacobs/jacobs.html.
6. Redpath, *The Roving Editor*, 141.
7. Even Jacobs turned to "amalgamation," beginning a relationship with one slaveholder in order to protect herself from another.
8. Tera W. Hunter, *Bound in Wedlock* (Cambridge, MA: Harvard University Press, 2017), 10, Kindle edition.
9. Slave ships continued to trickle in after the 1808 ban.
10. Thomas Jefferson, letter to John Wayles Eppes, June 30, 1820, https:// tjrs.monticello.org/letter/380#X3184701.
11. Karen Cook Bell, *Running from Bondage* (New York: Cambridge University Press, 2021), 25, Kindle edition.

12. "Sales and Separations," Hidden Voices: Enslaved Women in the Low-country and U.S. South, LDHI, https://ldhi.library.cofc.edu/exhibits/show/hidden-voices/enslaved-women-and-slaveholder/sales-and-separations.

13. Henry Bibb, *Narrative of the Life and Adventures of Henry Bibb, an American Slave, Written by Himself* (New York, 1849; Documenting the American South, 2000), 38.

14. Bibb, *Narrative of the Life*, 40.

15. Thomas L. Webber, *Deep Like the Rivers: Education in the Slave Quarter Community, 1831–1865* (New York: W. W. Norton, 1978), 105.

16. Henry Bibb, *Narrative of the Life and Adventures of Henry Bibb, An American Slave, Written by Himself* (New York: Henry Bibb, 1849), 189.

17. Bibb, *Life and Adventures of Henry Bibb*, 189.

18. Bibb, 190.

19. Bibb, 191.

20. Thomas A. Foster, *Rethinking Rufus* (Georgia: University of Georgia Press, 2019), 21.

21. Hunter, *Bound in Wedlock*, 6–7, Kindle edition.

22. Bell, *Running from Bondage*, 22, Kindle edition.

23. James T. Johnson, "English Puritan Thought on the Ends of Marriage," *Church History* 38, no. 4 (1969): 429–36, https://doi.org/10.2307/3163518.

24. Thomas Paine, "African Slavery in America," *Pennsylvania Journal and the Weekly Advertiser*, March 8, 1775, http://www.thomas-paine-friends.org/paine-thomas_african-slavery-in-america-1775.htm.

25. Danielle McGuire, *At the Dark End of the Street: Black Women, Rape, and Resistance—A New History of the Civil Rights Movement from Rosa Parks to the Rise of Black Power* (New York: Vintage Books, 2011), xviii.

26. McGuire, *At the Dark End of the Street*, xix.

27. McGuire, 181–82.

28. McGuire, 183.

29. "Racial Inequity and the Death Penalty, Past and Present," Equal Justice USA, https://ejusa.org/wp-content/uploads/EJUSA-DP-factsheet-race.pdf.

Chapter Five "Not a Single Presbyterian Negro"

1. "Kind but Blind: Southern Churches and Slavery, 1850s," BibleMesh, February 25, 2020, https://biblemesh.com/blog/kind-but-blind-southern-churches-and-slavery-1850s/.

2. Katharine Gerbner, *Christian Slavery*, Early American Studies (Philadelphia: University of Pennsylvania Press, 2018), 13, Kindle edition.

3. Paul Harvey, *Through the Storm, Through the Night*, The African American Experience Series (Plymouth: Rowman & Littlefield, 2011), 29, Kindle edition.

4. Harvey, *Through the Storm*, 30, Kindle edition.

5. Alpert, "The Origin of Slavery."

6. Gerbner, *Christian Slavery*, 115, Kindle edition.

7. It's important to note that other slaveholding countries—England, France, Spain, and Portugal—saw missionary endeavors toward the enslaved as an important side "benefit" of chattel slavery, as Albert J. Raboteau points out in *Slave Religion* (New York: Oxford University Press, 1978), 97. America would eventually take the same opinion.

8. Harvey, *Through the Storm*, 46–47, Kindle edition.

9. Daniel A. Payne, "Slavery Brutalizes Man" (speech, Franckean Synod, Fordsboro, NY, June 1839), https://www.blackpast.org/african-american-hi story/1839-daniel-payne-slavery-brutalizes-man/.

10. Payne, "Slavery Brutalizes Man."

11. Choreplscopus, "The Moral Character of Slavery: Letters from a Clergyman," *Richmond Courier*, May 23, 1851, https://chroniclingamerica.loc .gov/data/batches/vi_blass_ver01/data/sn84024735/00415664321/1851052301 /0240.pdf.

12. Payne, "Slavery Brutalizes Man."

13. General Assembly is an annual assemblage of Presbyterian churches. Resolutions that impact the denomination are discussed and voted upon.

14. "Ecclesiastical Relation of Negroes," Synod of Virginia, November 9, 1867, 3, https://en.wikisource.org/wiki/Ecclesiastical_Relation_of_Negroes.

15. Robert Lewis Dabney, "Speech on the Ecclesiastical Relation of Negroes," presented in the Synod of Virginia, November 9, 1867 (Richmond: The Boys and Girls Monthly, 1868), 5, https://en.wikisource.org/wiki/Eccle siastical_Relation_of_Negroes.

16. Charles W. Gardner, speech at the Fourth Annual Report of the American Anti-Slavery Society, May 9, 1837, https://libraries.udmercy.edu/archives /special-collections/index.php?record_id=2304&collectionCode=baa&item _id=2692.

17. Malcolm X, *The Autobiography of Malcolm X* (New York: Random House, 1964), 7, 4, 202–3, Kindle edition.

18. Henry Highland Garnet, "Let the Monster Perish" (speech, Capitol Building, Washington, DC, February 12, 1865), https://www.blackpast.org /african-american-history/1865-henry-highland-garnet-let-monster-perish/.

19. Henry Highland Garnet, "Call to Rebellion: An Address to the Slaves of the United States of America," Africans in America, August 21, 1843, PBS, https://www.pbs.org/wgbh/aia/part4/4h2937t.html.

20. Thomas C. Oden, *How Africa Shaped the Christian Mind: Rediscovering the African Seedbed of Western Christianity* (Downers Grove: InterVarsity, 2007), 42–44, Kindle edition.

21. Oden, *How Africa Shaped the Christian Mind*, 89–91, Kindle edition.

Chapter Six "Slavery Has Well Nigh Murdered Him"

1. Samuel Cartwright, "Diseases and Peculiarities of the Negro Race," *De Bow's Review* 11 (1851), Africans in America, https://www.pbs.org/wgbh /aia/part4/4h3106t.html.

2. Cartwright, "Diseases and Peculiarities."

3. Harriet Jacobs (Linda Brent), "The Fugitive Slave Law," chap. 40 in *Incidents in the Life of a Slave Girl: Written by Herself*, last updated December 18, 1997, http://xroads.virginia.edu/~Hyper/JACOBS1/hjch40.htm.

4. Charlotte Forten Grimké, *The Journal of Charlotte Forten Grimké* (New York: Dryden Press, 1953), 69.

5. Slave Power here does not refer to the enslaved as powerful but, rather, the power of Southern slaveholders to advance their slaveholding cause across America.

6. The Forten family pastor was Daniel Payne, who declared that "slavery brutalizes man."

7. Charlotte Grimké, *Journal of Charlotte Forten Grimké*, 70.

8. William Watkins, "Editorial, March 4, 1854," *Black Abolitionist Papers*, vol. 4 (Chapel Hill, NC: University of North Carolina Press, 1991), 228–29.

9. Francis James Grimké, *Victory for the Allies and the United States a Ground of Rejoicing, of Thanksgiving*, 1918, https://www.blackpast.org/african-american-history/1918-rev-francis-j-grimke-victory-allies-and-united-states-ground-rejoicing-thanksgiving/#:~:text=But%20the%20simple%20fact%20is,government%20under%20which%20he%20lives.

10. Francis Grimké, *Victory for the Allies*.

11. Francis J. Grimké, letter to Woodrow Wilson, Washington DC, November 20, 1912.

Chapter Seven Frater-Feeling

1. Jane Rhodes, *Mary Ann Shadd Cary: The Black Press and Protest in the Nineteenth Century* (Bloomington, IN: Indiana University Press, 1999), 21.

2. Rhodes, *Mary Ann Shadd Cary*.

3. *Maryland Colonization Journal* vol. 5, no. 3 (September 1849), https://static1.squarespace.com/static/590be125ff7c502a07752a5b/t/5c55b8bb9140b73529931e4a/1549121723752/Garnet%2C+Henry+Highland%2C+August+31%2C+1849+Letter+From+Garnet+to+Frederick+Douglass.pdf.

4. "How These Brethren Love One Another," *Maryland Colonization Journal*, September 1849, https://static1.squarespace.com/static/590be125ff7c502a07752a5b/t/5c55b8bb9140b73529931e4a/1549121723752/Garnet%2C+Henry+Highland%2C+August+31%2C+1849+Letter+From+Garnet+to+Frederick+Douglass.pdf.

5. Sidney Levy, "The Rise of the African Methodist Episcopal Church in Baltimore and the Bethel A.M.E. Church," Maryland Center for History and Culture, https://www.mdhistory.org/the-rise-of-the-african-methodist-episcopal-church-in-baltimore-and-the-bethel-a-m-e-church/.

6. Stewart, "Why Sit Ye Here and Die?"

7. Maria W. Stewart (speech, Afric-American Female Intelligence Society of Boston, Boston, MA, April 28, 1832), https://awpc.cattcenter.iastate.edu/2020/11/20/an-address-april-28-1832/.

8. Maria W. Stewart, "Mrs. Stewart's Farewell Address to Her Friends in the City of Boston" (Boston, MA, September 21, 1833), https://awpc.cattcenter .iastate.edu/2020/11/20/mrs-stewarts-farewell-address-to-her-friends-in-the -city-of-boston-sept-21-1833/.

9. Jarena Lee, *Religious Experience and Journal of Mrs. Jarena Lee, Giving an Account of Her Call to Preach the Gospel* (Philadelphia: Pantianos Classics, 1836), 11–12, Kindle edition.

10. Yee, *Black Women Abolitionists*, 49, 50, 56.

11. J. W. C. Pennington, quoted in Daniel Payne, *History of the African Methodist Episcopal Church* (Nashville: Publishing House of the AME Sunday School Union, 1891), 301.

12. Frederick Douglass, "What the Black Man Wants" (speech, Annual Meeting of the Massachusetts Anti-Slavery Society, 1865), https://www.black past.org/african-american-history/1865-frederick-douglass-what-black-man -wants/.

13. Frances Ellen Watkins Harper, "We Are All Bound Up Together" (speech, Eleventh National Women's Rights Convention, New York, May 1866), https://www.blackpast.org/african-american-history/speeches-afric an-american-history/1866-frances-ellen-watkins-harper-we-are-all-bound -together/#:~:text=You%20white%20women%20speak%20here,every%2 0man's%20hand%20against%20me.

14. Sojourner Truth, "Address to the First Annual Meeting of the American Equal Rights Association," Society for the Study of American Women Writers (New York City, May 9, 1867), https://www.lehigh.edu/~dek7/SSAWW /writTruthAddress.htm; "Why the Women's Rights Movement Split over the 15th Amendment," National Park Service, last updated January 14, 2021, https://www.nps.gov/articles/000/why-the-women-s-rights-movement-split -over-the-15th-amendment.htm.

15. Sally Loomis, "The Evolution of Paul Cuffe's Black Nationalism," *Negro History Bulletin* 37, no. 6 (1974): 298–302, http://www.jstor.org/stable/4417 5197.

16. "Overlooked No More: How Mary Ann Shadd Cary Shook Up the Abolitionist Movement," *New York Times*, https://www.nytimes.com/2018 /06/06/obituaries/mary-ann-shadd-cary-abolitionist-overlooked.html.

17. Mary Ann Shadd, "Break Every Yoke and Let the Oppressed Go Free" (sermon, Chatham, Canada, April 6, 1858), https://www.blackpast .org/global-african-history/1858-mary-ann-shadd-break-every-yoke-and-let -oppressed-go-free/.

18. Jennifer Lund Smith, "Lucy Craft Laney and Martha Berry," in *Georgia Women: Their Lives and Times*, vol. 1, ed. Ann Short Chirhart and Betty Wood, Southern Women: Their Lives and Times (Athens, GA: University of Georgia Press, 2009), loc. 4771–74, Kindle edition.

19. Loomis, "Evolution of Paul Cuffe's Black Nationalism," 298.

20. "Biography that idealizes its subject" (*Oxford English Dictionary*).

Chapter Eight "God Gave Me That Freedom"

1. John Murray (Lord Dunmore), "Lord Dunmore's Proclamation, 1775," *Pennsylvania Journal and Weekly Advertiser*, The Gilder Lehrman Institute of American History, December 6, 1775, https://www.gilderlehrman.org/history -resources/spotlight-primary-source/lord-dunmores-proclamation-1775.

2. Murray, "Lord Dunmore's Proclamation."

3. Laura Eliza Wilkes, *Missing Pages in American History* (Washington, DC: RL Pendleton, 1919), 50.

4. Bell, *Running from Bondage*, 161, Kindle edition.

5. Amy Post, postscript to Jacobs, *Incidents in the Life*, 305.

6. Camp, *Closer to Freedom*, 35–59, Kindle edition.

7. David Wilmot, *Congressional Globe, 29th Congress, 2nd sess.*, 1847, appendix, 317; reprinted in William E. Gienapp, ed., *The Civil War and Reconstruction: A Documentary Collection* (New York: W. W. Norton, 2001), 17–18, https://shec.ashp.cuny.edu/items/show/1247#:~:text=The%20amend ment%20came%20to%20be,the%20rights%20of%20white%20freemen.

8. *The Dred Scott Decision: Opinion of Chief Justice Taney* (New York: Van Evrie, Horton & Co., 1860), image 18, https://www.loc.gov/resource /llst.022/?sp=18&st=text.

9. "Confederate States of America—Declaration of the Immediate Causes Which Induce and Justify the Secession of South Carolina from the Federal Union," The Avalon Project, December 24, 1860, https://avalon.law.yale.edu /19th_century/csa_scarsec.asp.

10. "Confederate States of America."

11. "A Declaration of the Causes Which Impel the State of Texas to Secede from the Federal Union," Texas State Library and Archives Commission, February 2, 1861, https://www.tsl.texas.gov/ref/abouttx/secession/2feb1861.html.

12. Alexander H. Stephens, "The Corner Stone Speech" (speech, Savannah, GA, March 21, 1861), https://iowaculture.gov/sites/default/files/history -education-pss-civil-cornerstone-transcription.pdf.

13. James W. Loewen and Edward H. Sebesta, *The Confederate and Neo-Confederate Reader: The "Great Truth" about the "Lost Cause"* (Jackson: University Press of Mississippi, 2010), 33, Kindle edition.

14. Abraham Lincoln, "A Letter from the President: To Hon. Horace Greeley," *Daily National Intelligencer*, Washington, DC, August 23, 1862, https:// www.loc.gov/resource/mal.4233400/?st=text.

15. Locke himself, though not a slaveholder, was a stockholder in the Royal African Company, which had a monopoly on the slave trade.

16. Loewen and Sebesta, *Confederate and Neo-Confederate Reader*, 63, Kindle edition.

17. "Living Contraband: Former Slaves in the Nation's Capital during the Civil War," National Park Service, https://www.nps.gov/articles/living -contraband-former-slaves-in-the-nation-s-capital-during-the-civil-war.htm.

18. Camp, *Closer to Freedom*, 118, Kindle edition.

19. James Barbot, quoted in Rebecca Hall, *Wake: The Hidden History of Women-Led Slave Revolts* (New York: Simon & Schuster, 2021).

Chapter Nine "As Scarce as Hen's Teeth"

1. It's important to note that Christianity was not the only religion practiced by the enslaved. That is *this* researcher's particular focus, but not the only expression that existed on the plantation. Often, enslaved Africans brought the faiths of their homeland to American shores, or mixed elements of African spiritualism with their Christian or Muslim expressions in the U.S.

2. Thomas Johnson, *Twenty-Eight Years a Slave* (London: Alexander & Shepheard, 1892), 12.

3. Janet Duitsman Cornelius, *When I Can Read My Title Clear* (Columbia, SC: University of South Carolina Press, 1992), 33.

4. Cornelius, *When I Can Read*, 34.

5. Johnson, *Twenty-Eight Years*, 18.

6. Peter Rudolph, quoted in Webber, *Deep Like the Rivers*, 97.

7. Johnson, *Twenty-Eight Years*, 13.

8. Cornelius, *When I Can Read*, 25.

9. Johnson, *Twenty-Eight Years*, 17.

10. Josiah Henson, *The Life of Josiah Henson, Formerly a Slave, Now an Inhabitant of Canada, as Narrated by Himself* (Boston: Arter D. Phelps, 1849), 11, https://docsouth.unc.edu/neh/henson49/henson49.html.

11. John Brown, *Slave Life in Georgia* (London: WM Watts, 1855), 202, https://docsouth.unc.edu/neh/jbrown/jbrown.html.

12. William Craft, *Running a Thousand Miles for Freedom* (London: William Tweedie, 1860), 10.

13. Frances Ellen Watkins Harper and Koritha Mitchell, *Iola Leroy: or, Shadows Uplifted* (Ontario, Canada: Broadview Press, 2018), 11–12, Kindle edition.

14. Webber, *Deep Like Rivers*, 86.

15. Aaron Siddles, quoted in Webber, *Deep Like Rivers*, 84.

16. Webber, *Deep Like Rivers*, 99.

17. Webber, 99.

18. Webber, 99.

19. Webber, 98.

20. Heather Andrea Williams, "'Clothing Themselves in Intelligence': The Freedpeople, Schooling, and Northern Teachers, 1861–1871," *Journal of African American History* 87 (2002): 372–89, https://doi.org/10.2307/1562471.

21. Ida B. Wells, *Crusade for Justice: The Autobiography of Ida B. Wells*, ed. Alfreda M. Duster (Chicago: University of Chicago Press, 1970, 2020), 154–55.

22. Frances Ellen Watkins, "Liberty for Slaves" (speech, Maine Anti-Slavery Society, 1857), https://www.blackpast.org/african-american-history/1857-frances-ellen-watkins-liberty-slaves/.

Chapter Ten "The Rights Which Manhood Can Confer"

1. D. W. Griffith, *The Rise and Fall of Free Speech in America* (Los Angeles: Griffith, 1916), 27.

2. Though Woodrow Wilson's famously attributed quote about the film ("It's like writing history with lightning. My only regret is that it is all so terribly true.") might never have been said, he did give the film his tacit approval by allowing it to be viewed at the White House. Mark E. Benbow, "Birth of a Quotation: Woodrow Wilson and 'Like Writing History with Lightning,'" *Journal of the Gilded Age and Progressive Era* 9, no. 4 (2010): 509–33, http://www.jstor.org/stable/20799409.

3. Charles W. Puttkammer and Ruth Worthy, "William Monroe Trotter, 1872–1934," *Journal of Negro History* 43, no. 4 (1958): 298–316, https://doi.org/10.2307/2716146.

4. Griffith, *Rise and Fall*, 31.

5. "The Caning of Senator Charles Sumner," United States Senate, May 22, 1856, https://www.senate.gov/artandhistory/history/minute/The_Caning_of_Senator_Charles_Sumner.htm.

6. Charles Sumner, *The Crime Against Kansas* (1856; repr., Hardpress, 2013), 11.

7. "Landmark Legislation: Civil Rights Act of 1875," United States Senate, https://www.senate.gov/artandhistory/history/common/generic/CivilRightsAct1875.htm.

8. And they were excuses. It's important to note that I am not arguing that Du Bois, Washington, or Douglass were "less" Black because of their white ancestry.

9. Robert Elliott (speech, Congress, January 6, 1874), quoted in Robert Brammer, "When the Former Vice President of the Confederacy Debated Civil Rights with an African American Congressman," Library of Congress, July 22, 2020, https://blogs.loc.gov/law/2020/07/when-the-former-vice-president-of-the-confederacy-debated-civil-rights-with-an-african-american-congressman/.

10. Alexander H. Stephens, "Cornerstone Speech" (speech, Savannah, GA, March 21, 1861), https://www.battlefields.org/learn/primary-sources/cornerstone-speech.

11. Robert B. Elliot, "Neglected Voices: Speeches of African-American Representatives Addressing the Civil Rights Bill of 1875" (speech, January 6, 1874), 7, http://www.law.nyu.edu/sites/default/files/civilrightsactspeeches.pdf.

12. "Landmark Legislation: Civil Rights Act of 1875."

13. Joseph H. Rainey, "Neglected Voices: Speeches of African-American Representatives Addressing the Civil Rights Bill of 1875" (speech, December 19, 1873), http://www.law.nyu.edu/sites/default/files/civilrightsactspeeches.pdf.

14. Richard H. Cain, "Neglected Voices: Speeches of African-American Representatives Addressing the Civil Rights Bill of 1875" (speech, January 10,

1854), 29, http://www.law.nyu.edu/sites/default/files/civilrightsactspeeches .pdf.

15. Henry Louis Gates Jr., "Which Slave Sailed Himself to Freedom?," *The African Americans: Many Rivers to Cross*, https://www.pbs.org/wnet /african-americans-many-rivers-to-cross/history/which-slave-sailed-himself -to-freedom/.

16. Booker T. Washington, "Atlanta Compromise" (speech, Cotton States and International Exposition, Atlanta, GA, September 18, 1895), http://his torymatters.gmu.edu/d/39/.

17. "Booker T. Washington and the 'Atlanta Compromise,'" National Museum of African American History and Culture, https://nmaahc.si.edu /explore/stories/booker-t-washington-and-atlanta-compromise.

18. "Booker T. Washington."

Afterword

1. They absolutely did—Charles Spurgeon's sermons were burned in the South because of his vocal protestation against slavery.

ACKNOWLEDGMENTS

As ever, I am grateful for my husband, Phillip, without whom this book would not be possible. He thinks I can do anything and shows it in his support.

I researched and wrote this book in a huge black recliner in the corner of his office, often nursing a newborn while I balanced books on my knees. There would have been very little book-balancing *or* nursing without my mother-in-law's help around my house and with my toddler.

Wynn, Langston, and Jamie, for the life-giving snugs and constant interruptions—I will miss you when you're not stopping me in the middle of edits for hugs.

Patnacia Goodman always sees the vision—even when I falter. She is a dream of an editor and a hype woman.

Collin Huber is *also* a dream of an editor and has made almost all of my books sing.

Dr. Abena Ansah-Wright has always made me feel like a scholar as I pursue the answer to my historical inquiries. She helps me grapple with the sources and always has a book recommendation for my rabbit holes. And she's excellent at babysitting me during an all-out writer meltdown, for which I am thankful.

Speaking of my meltdowns—Keydra Garner and Portia Collins, thank you ever so much for helping me through those.

To each and every friend—your support means the most.

I am rather partial to Black women historians, and there were a lot of them involved in my reading for this book: Martha S. Jones, Karen Cook Bell, Rebecca Hall, Kerri K. Greenidge, Annette Gordon-Reed, Stephanie Camp, Tera W. Hunter, Deborah Gray White, Darlene Clark Hine, just to name a few . . . their work brought history to life for me, and made me want to bring it to life for others.

JASMINE L. HOLMES is a passionate writer and educator who celebrates Black stories through her books and public history resources. With a love for literature and academic rigor, she immerses herself in research to uncover the hidden narratives that shape our world. Her commitment to centering Black experiences shines through in her writing, which includes the books *Carved in Ebony* and *Mother to Son*. As a research assistant and teacher, Jasmine shares her expertise with lifelong learners and educators alike, inspiring them to expand their understanding of history and its impact on our society. Alongside her husband and three sons, Jasmine calls Jackson, Mississippi, home. Learn more at www.JasmineLHolmes.com and connect with her on Instagram @JasmineLHolmes.